apartment
therapy's
big book of
small, cool
spaces

apartment therapy's big book of small, cool spaces

MAXWELL GILLINGHAM-RYAN

Clarkson Potter/Publishers
New York

PAGE 1 The entrance to this remarkable cherry staircase makes itself smaller and provides an air of privacy with a veil of wood, while amplifying the wide landing.

PREVIOUS SPREAD This Brooklyn office was designed as a personal retreat by the owner, a writer, who works from home. It sits on the top floor, drawing plenty of light from the windows on the right to illuminate the many books and glowing white Corian desktop housed amidst the custom bamboo cabinetry.

THIS PAGE With the parents' bedroom in the loft upstairs, the childrens' room glows with warmth below in this very modern renovation.

Library of Congress Cataloging-in-Publication Data

Gillingham-Ryan, Maxwell.
   Apartment therapy's big book of small, cool spaces / Maxwell Gillingham-Ryan. — 1st ed.
      p.   cm.
   Big book of small, cool spaces
   Includes index.
1. Small rooms—Decoration.   I. Title.
   NK2117.S59G56 2010
   747—dc22   2009028199

ISBN 978-0-307-46460-6

Printed in China

Design by Jennifer K. Beal Davis

Photographs by Jim Franco

10 9 8 7 6 5 4 3 2 1

First Edition

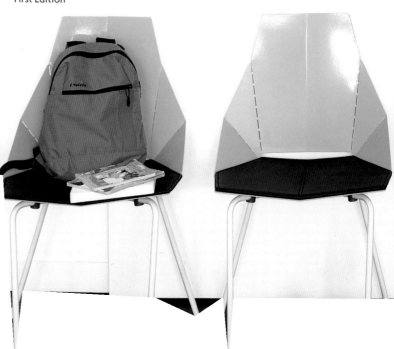

For the people in this book
who welcomed me into
their homes and for
Sara Kate and Ursula who
help me make mine

contents

introduction

NOTHING YOU DO FOR YOUR HOME IS EVER WASTED.

I love figuring out how to make a room work. I have always been obsessed with beautiful and comfortable homes, with trying to figure out what makes them tick and helping to create them.

When I was about twelve, my mother told me I could do anything I wanted with my room, and I spent months drawing elaborate plans on paper. My bed was going to sit at the bottom of a smooth bowl (early skate-park influence), at the top of a set of stairs; it was all going to be made of plywood, covered with padding and carpeting. As soon as my plans were done, I began working on improvements, and my vision got more complicated and more fabulous with each iteration. While my room didn't actually change that much in the end, my research had definitely begun.

Now I decorate and reenvision rooms for a living, and the more spaces I've seen, the more I've become convinced that there are basic lessons and common elements that make a room great—lessons that are not hard to learn and that don't require a substantial amount of money to implement.

ABOVE This stylish wall unit is a great example of design solving the space problem. The wall provides tons of clothing and book storage as well as housing a full office along a very thin slice of this studio apartment.

Ever since I started working with clients, in 2001, this has been the focus of Apartment Therapy: distilling the most common problems and finding solutions that are transformative, stylish, and often surprisingly easy to carry out.

People come to me with their problems, as they would to a therapist, and of all the home-related problems I've heard, the most common one is lack of space. Most people who say they can't create the home they want claim it's because they require more room. "My place just isn't big enough" and "I can't wait until I move and have more space" are common refrains. If you've picked up this book, there's a good chance that you, too, are looking for solutions to the "problem" of your limited space.

You may not have a small home, but nearly all of us around the world have at least one small room that we don't know how to handle, such as an entryway or a galley kitchen. In interior design, "big" is not our common language—"small" is.

In addition to living in a series of small homes—including the 250-square-foot one-bedroom apartment I shared with my wife and young

ABOVE RIGHT Playing with scale is one of the secrets to enlivening and enlarging a small space. These quirky, personal objects on a mantelpiece draw us in close, while the large mirror above directs our gaze away.

daughter—I've had the pleasure of visiting a lot of homes and have been inspired by how inventive and efficient small-space dwellers are. They also are among the most passionate. Proud of what they've done, small-space lovers are natural designers, constantly reworking their homes and figuring out how to do more with less. New design discoveries arise with every new challenge.

In 2004, ApartmentTherapy.com launched the first annual Smallest Coolest Home Contest. It was an idea born of my own situation, inspired by the experience of stumbling upon surprising jewel-box homes tucked into New York City's canyons, and hearing urban legends of people who had transformed water towers into tiny apartments that you could reach only by climbing a ladder. Five years later the contest has grown exponentially and surpassed my wildest dreams. We now receive hundreds of entries from all over the world: from Boston, Pasadena, and Iowa City to Vienna, Hong Kong, Buenos Aires, and Bangalore. Every home is full of passion, hard work, and amazing creativity.

Inspired by all of this, when the idea for this book first arose, I resisted a concept I'd seen so often before: a bunch of impersonal, staged rooms. I wanted to dig up small homes with uniqueness and character, homes that are truly lived-in, ones you don't often see. And I wanted to personally visit them, so that I could unpack their secrets firsthand.

Indirect light is crucial. The double lamps on the small vintage record cabinet provide half of the light for this dining room. Stylish black shades and two mourning doves complete the vignette.

Home pleasures can be simple pleasures. This vintage cup, spoon, and rose fabric make the room feel cozy and invite one to stay home, have tea, and curl up with a book.

In the end, I spent weeks on the road, followed up on nearly two hundred leads, and visited thirty handpicked homes. I spent hours in each place, asking questions, taking notes, and, occasionally, sharing a meal as well. Formerly the guru, I was now the student, listening to others tell me about their amazing spaces and how they'd done it all. I loved it.

I'm looking forward to taking you with me to see the minuscule bedroom with a four-poster bed that gives it a surprising scale and air of grandeur. I want to show you a studio apartment whose owner found room for a kitchen by placing it beneath a bed. I want to teach you how to make the most remarkable ceiling-mounted dividers—sheer curtains that turn one room into four. And I want to share a fabulous corner office that disappears in an instant behind two antique French glass doors in a dreamy white bedroom.

Welcome to my *Big Book of Small, Cool Spaces.* If you struggle with your space, you will find kinship in these pages—and lots of new ideas, too. If you are living large and want to pare down, or have a problem in one of your rooms, you will find inspiration and a new perspective. From coast to coast, here are rooms that will speak to you, lessons that will stay with you, and people who will encourage you to get working on your home right now, no matter how much room you have.

HOW THIS BOOK WORKS

This book is meant to be easy to dive into and really useful. After all, I want you to get so excited that you'll eventually put it down.

Each self-contained chapter focuses on a different space, such as the entrance or the bedroom, moving you through the home, literally from front to back. You can read straight through or start in the middle; you'll never get lost.

Each chapter begins with general thoughts and tips for making the most of that particular space, followed by a half-dozen or more in-depth room dissections that detail why each one works so well. The sources for each can be found in the back of the book.

OPPOSITE Good ideas are everywhere. Although a contractor built these boxes, affordable, off-the-rack versions or display shelves could be arranged in a similar formation to re-create the look.

Aside from the detailed room studies, each chapter also contains my thoughts on various subjects that are important to those rooms and to small spaces, such as lighting, bookshelves, and wall colors. These sections specifically focus on design features that not only optimize square footage, but are stylish as well.

Finally, in addition to the extensive resource listings at the end of the book, I've inserted my own lists of highly recommended resources throughout for easy reference and to jump-start your own research on the Web, where the Apartment Therapy community and I gather daily.

As you read this book I hope you will experience the pleasure that all these folks have had in working on their homes, making the most of some really challenging spaces. I hope it will inspire you to try to rearrange your bedroom so it feels huge or to cut an old table in half to make yourself a landing strip for your entrance. When you start rolling up your sleeves and working with your home, it is truly energizing. You'll get a great feeling from discovering that so much is possible and that your space can seem so much bigger than you thought. Enjoy!

ABOVE I love open storage. While it's easy for it to end up looking messy, streamlined coordinated dishware makes for a cohesive, considered display in a kitchen.

■ TIP Choosing dishware in a color that blends or contrasts with the wall behind it adds even more sophistication.

OPPOSITE A classic way to maximize space, loft beds figure prominently in this book. Here, a consistent, warm color palette throughout the room lets the loft frame blend in seamlessly. The slim, strong plumber's pipe used for the railing and the translucent carpet protector within allow copious light to reach the bedroom from the windows.

quick
entrances

In ancient Greece, the entrance was more than just the passage into a home; it was also a spiritual space for residents to shed the layers (and cares) of public life before entering the private quarters to relax and tend to the domestic side of life. I love this concept and firmly believe it is just as important in a modern home as it was way back then. It's not just about having a place to leave your boots and umbrellas: The entrance, no matter what its size, allows you a moment for an emotional transition as well.

Unfortunately, small homes typically have very little room for entrances, and it is easy to fall into thinking that planning for one is impossible. But a good entrance doesn't require a lot of space.

PREVIOUS PAGE This apartment is actually in an old factory space, so it is an understatement to say that it lacked an entrance—it lacked anything even remotely residential! To give the large space around the metal doorway a warm feeling and a usable landing strip, the owner stacked old steamer trunks (which double as storage) next to a funky chair.

ABOVE This front hallway started as just a wall with an interrupting fuse box and intercom. The addition of a wall mount cabinet creates a landing strip and storage, while the collection of artwork cleverly hides the offending utilities.

The fundamental thing that every entrance needs is a "landing strip" containing three things:

1. A place to drop your keys, cell phone, and mail as you come in, to keep this stuff from flooding other rooms.

2. A mirror for quick visual checks before you head out for the evening or go off to work.

3. At least two hooks, so that anyone who visits your home has a handy (and tidy) place to stash his or her coat.

Outfitted in this way, the entrance performs another vital function—that of a filter. It helps keep your outside stuff organized so that it doesn't clutter the inside of your apartment. Here are a few more general tips for creating the best entryway for a small space.

- MOVE OUTSIDE FOR MORE ROOM. There's no rule that says your landing strip must start inside your home: To get more space and enlarge your entrance, put your doormat outside your door—in a communal hallway, if you have one, or in an enclosed porch—and install a hook and a shoe rack nearby for daily-use items.

ABOVE Along with the lovely oval mirror, this vintage cabinet doubles as a landing strip and art display, with a welcoming wave each time you enter the door.

OPPOSITE This small dining table beside the front door is where keys and mail land and get sorted, but it also can host dinner for four when necessary.

- GET THE PERFECT HALL TABLE. Finding a long, narrow console table that fits both the dimensions and the style of a small entrance is hard. One way to expand your options dramatically: Buy a table you like at a flea market and cut it in half, lengthwise, then attach the cut side to the wall with two small, strong brackets. It just might become the coolest thing in your home.

- TAKE ADVANTAGE OF A STYLE OPPORTUNITY. Remember that your entrance is the first part of your home that any guest will see, so it plays a large role in setting the mood. Small personal items like photographs, artwork, decorative bowls, and plants will make an impact and enrich the space.

THE LONG HOUSE ENTRANCE

Although the narrow, runway-style hallways common to many apartment buildings can be challenging to work with, they offer lots of wall space to hold daily essentials. The more that is added to the walls, though, the busier they get, so it's important to be careful with the placement of objects. Here, one owner is an interior designer and the other is an architect, so it's not surprising that they found a great solution for their narrow entrance.

■ LAYOUT—The owners turned their long, rectangular space from a challenge into an asset. Rather than try to squeeze a coatrack and a sideboard right next to the doorway, they used a row of coat hooks (and a consistent paint color) to extend the experience of the hallway from the door to a cutback in the wall a few feet away that made a perfect spot for a larger-scale landing strip.

LEFT This coatrack's organic shape contrasts nicely with the apartment's modern architecture and puts the narrowest part of the hallway to work.

■ TIP Mount multiple identical racks in the same area for added, sculptural drama.

RIGHT A collection of young artists' works is clustered together in an assortment of frames—most streamlined and minimal, but with a few ornate pieces thrown into the mix. The casual arrangement lets the couple integrate some functional features (like the intercom and the fuse box) without having to cover them completely.

OWNERS
Vané and Chad Broussard

PROFESSIONS
Interior designer and
blogger (Vané); Archi-
tectural designer (Chad)

LOCATION
Brooklyn Heights, New York

TYPE
Studio, 500 square feet

■ STYLE—Vané's style is bright, colorful, and handcrafted, while Chad's is
more minimal and modern. Both work together nicely here. The white,
minimal elements open up the space and make it appear uncluttered,
while the green accents (the fabric runner, some of the artwork) draw
attention and add liveliness.

This apartment is really small, and a great deal has been fit into it. In a
later chapter you will see the adjacent living room, which contains two
offices as well as the bedroom (see page 113). Built-in cabinets are the best
way to maximize space, because they waste none and can be camouflaged
easily. They also can be expensive, but with IKEA cabinets the same effect
can be achieved in a number of ways.

RENTERS
Michelle and Tracy
McCormick

PROFESSIONS
Design director (Michelle);
Senior project manager
(Tracy)

LOCATION
Wilshire Boulevard, Los
Angeles

TYPE
One-bedroom, 875 square
feet

KEY INGREDIENTS
- Lots of mirrors
- Crystal chandelier
- Cowhide and kilim
  layered rugs

THE HALL OF MIRRORS

At first glance, it may seem that this entryway is a natural beauty, but that's only because the residents, Michelle and Tracy McCormick, have done such a nice job with it. True, the space itself is not tiny, but when the women moved into this historic Los Angeles apartment six years ago, the entrance was a dark and depressing nook.

What is especially amazing here is how the collections as a whole are used to enhance the space, while the individual pieces tell their own stories. It is easy to collect and create clutter, but in this hallway, the little assemblages of antique items sparkle and delight as the similarities among the grouped items and the care that has been taken with them reveal themselves.

- LAYOUT—This entrance lies right at the end of a long public hallway and is the center of the apartment, with passageways branching off for the kitchen and bedroom areas on either side. Michelle and Tracy have built upon this space's central role, creating a strong focal point right at the entrance with rugs, mirrors, and a statement-making chandelier.

- STYLE—The style here is definitely vintage, but time periods are inter-mixed. What pulls everything together are the groupings of similar objects (mirrors, mirror balls, frames, pinecones, pictures of cowboys) and the groupings of color (reflective, brown, and white). This thematic unity keeps the room from feeling crowded, as do the white surrounding walls. Most of the rooms in this apartment are painted with dark colors, so the white also emphasizes the transition out of the entrance as you move forward.

ABOVE Limiting a vignette to a few materials—in this case, wood and metal—allows disparate shapes to coexist without seeming messy. Unlike many of the homes in this book, the bones of this one are very old. The residents have kept the character of the building alive by adding antique pieces that share the same prewar, premachine, handmade quality.

OPPOSITE The key to giving this once-neglected area presence and light was the collection of antique mirror balls and mirrored furniture—a perfect remedy for a dull space. And while one massive mirror can be prohibitively expensive, not to mention difficult to transport, here twenty smaller square mirrors have been cobbled together to create one large looking glass, whose subtle seams and irregularities echo the mirror balls.

When belongings are artfully arranged, display can take the place of storage. On the right side of the entrance, rather than try to find a large hidden spot for tucking away a regularly used surfboard, Michelle made it part of a 3-D scene, coupled with pared-down wooden furniture and black-and-white photographs.

This entryway provides multiple opportunities to give oneself a final once-over before heading out the door. The sizes and shapes of the mirror frames are all over the map, but the uniform shine brings them together.

RENTERS
Sara Kate and Maxwell
Gillingham-Ryan

PROFESSIONS
Food writer (Sara Kate);
Interior designer (Maxwell)

LOCATION
West Village, New York City

TYPE
Two-bedroom, 725 square
feet

KEY INGREDIENTS
- Free space outside the door
- Expandable shoe rack
- Large coir doormat

THE OUTSIDE ENTRANCE

This is our own entrance. Because the apartment is rather small and the front door opens right into the kitchen, I started our hallway outside our door, in the common space.

The extension happened unintentionally at first, when we began taking off our shoes before entering the house. Shoes are among the dirtiest things we bring inside, and if you make a habit of leaving them outside, not only will you keep your home cleaner, but your downstairs neighbors also will like you more (quieter footsteps). You may discover that socks are very good at keeping wood floors polished, and you will almost certainly find that your sense of space expands as you start to "come home" outside your door.

Not everyone has this option, and some buildings don't allow it, but it's a possibility worth looking into. If you live in a detached house, you can

ABOVE LEFT Our "entrance" is actually a little three-by-five-foot bit of room outside our door that holds everything we need. I hung a nice piece of artwork—best seen as you're coming up the stairs—to create a focal point. The doormat is of natural coir, and this one fills the space outside the door, blurring the indoor/outdoor boundaries.

■ **TIP** To restore paint-coated hooks to their original glory, boil them in water with baking soda for fifteen to twenty minutes. Most of the paint will fall right off. Vintage coat hooks are usually cheaper than new ones and add lots more character.

ABOVE LEFT A tiered shoe rack organizes footwear by owner—and a wooden clementine box corrals the littlest specimens. Even our daughter, Ursula, has a top shelf just for her own little shoes!

ABOVE RIGHT The large coat hooks are positioned so that you don't see them until you reach the top of the stairs. Bulkier items are hung here, but only the ones we use often. (We *do* have a coat closet inside our home for the rest of our less-used items.)

probably reclaim a lot of room outside your front door with just a few adjustments.

- LAYOUT—Our entrance is at the top of a narrow flight of stairs and on the way to the building's fire escape, so the space outside our door is rarely used by anyone but us. It is, however, visible to those below, so we keep it very neat.

- STYLE—Shoes can be messy, and so can coats, scarves, and all the stuff you end up dumping in a typical hallway. It is crucial to keep must-have outerwear pieces well edited and to have a designated space for each one. When using public space, respect your neighbors and keep it beautiful. We try not to overfill our shoe rack, coat hooks, or paper recycling basket, and we've made it easy to put things away on the fly. I find the old-fashioned concept of a jacket or scarf hanging on a hook by the front door not only practical, but also beautiful. Even when the clothing is not there, the hook itself can be good-looking.

LEFT At the entrance to this apartment, the ceiling drops down (supporting the loft bed), and the dark color of the wood makes it appear even lower, creating a cozy passage. It's here that the owners, Mark Robohm and Stephanie Doucette, pause and drop their keys, wallets, cell phones, and mail. Multiple inset light fixtures ensure that no portion of the hallway is left in shadow; arranged one after the other, they also subtly beckon visitors to travel into the home's main space.

OPPOSITE In a neat design detail, the ladder to the loft bed was built to disappear into the wall during the daytime, allowing for the hallway to remain clear.

THE HANDMADE HALLWAY

Visitors to this apartment enter a world in which almost everything has been made by hand—even the entryway itself. Originally laid out as an open-plan studio, the apartment didn't come with a defined entryway, so Mark and Stephanie created it, with both structural changes (building a loft bed over the area) and cosmetic ones. Capitalizing on the space's narrowness and length, they forged a functional hallway by building in a few stations that force you to pause along the way.

KEY INGREDIENTS:
- Tall ceilings
- Large hall console table
- Great shag rug

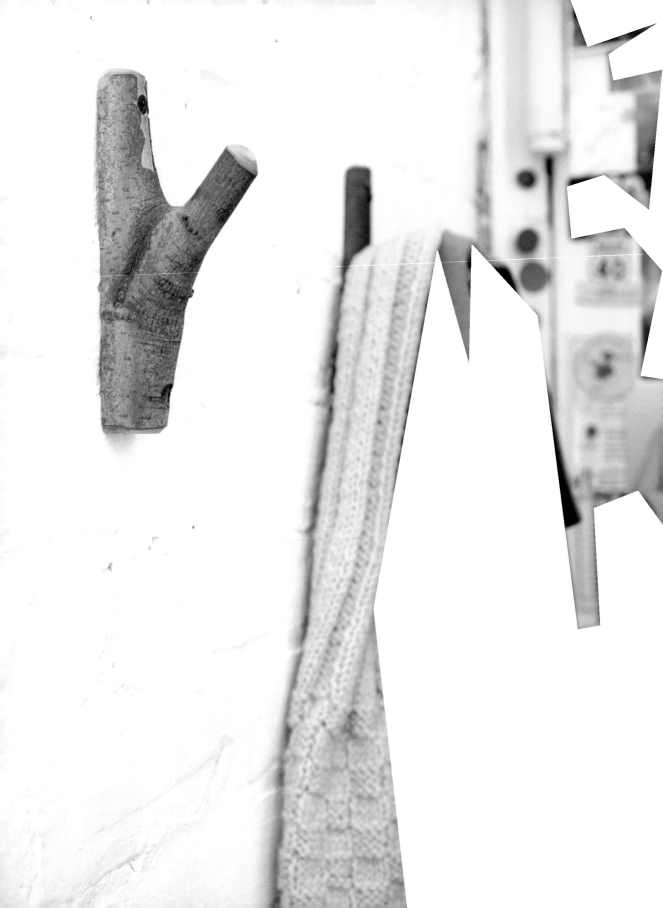

OPPOSITE Mark's father, a Vermont woodworker, made these twig-shaped scrap-timber hooks, and the dark walnut wood lining the walls came from the family's Vermont farm. These sentimental touches instantly and concretely set the tone for the apartment.

RIGHT The owners use small, plain magnets to layer their metal front door with family photos, travel mementos, and reminders. Coating a wooden door (or even a section of it) in magnetic paint is another way to create a backdrop for a constantly evolving personal collage.

- LAYOUT—The first area is marked off by a generously sized shag rug—a great way to focus a space. (Bonus: In addition to defining the area, the softness of a rug provides a gentle reminder of home each time someone walks through the door.) The higher ceiling in this first area allows the hooks and the tall mirror to be elevated on the wall, accentuating the extra space.

- STYLE—The style here is very personal. The owners use their entrance to surround themselves with reminders of family, friends, and other things that make them feel at home. A hallway like this is a great place to hang lots of photos, and it's okay if it ends up looking a little busy.

When Mark, who is a musician, isn't performing, he works on the apartment, taking care of everything from the electrical to woodwork to installing Sheetrock. His wife, Stephanie, a fashion designer, takes the lead when it comes to decorating, and together they've fashioned a home that is highly personal, inventive, and stylish at the same time.

OWNERS
Stephanie Doucette and Mark Robohm

PROFESSIONS
Drummer (Mark);
Dress designer (Stephanie)

LOCATION
Chelsea, New York City

TYPE
Two studios combined, for a total of 780 square feet

a few more
fast entrances

I called this chapter "Quick Entrances" because they really can be quick, and you can do great things with little handkerchiefs of room—or with no space at all—by maximizing the vertical space of your walls. Here are some more inventive solutions for particularly challenging spaces.

1. Go vertical. When floor space is tight, look for wall space to accommodate possessions vertically.

2. Fake it. Install a light or paint an accent wall to create an entrance where there is none.

3. Decor the door. Consider the front door a decorative opportunity—paint or cover it so that it can stand out or blend in.

4. Show storage. Turn storage into design by decoratively hanging a hat collection by the door.

5. Elevate your keys. Hang your keys by the door so you'll never lose them.

RIGHT Entrances are not only meant to be centers for efficiency, they also offer a chance to set a tone. Here, a few unexpected, artistic pieces add an element of delight and welcome to an otherwise forbidding entrance.

ABOVE Small, stylish key racks like this are growing in popularity. Many are magnetic, but some artfully ask the homeowner to stick his or her keys right into them. The one above is an oak slab called the Marvelous Key Rack and is designed by Tomke Biallas and Grisella Kreiterling.

OPPOSITE In a subtle but highly effective space-saving trick, this coatrack is mounted on the ceiling instead of on the wall behind the door, which preserves a precious extra few inches of clearance. The hat collection, evenly spaced on wall hooks, offers a pleasing and balanced focal point.

ABOVE This door led directly into a kitchen. For the owners, it was enough to use an adjacent shelf as a minimal landing strip, while covering the metal front door with upholstery fabric softened it and made it blend into the room.

RIGHT Here, the residents have maximized the all-too-often forgotten space behind their front door—and have managed to stash boots, jackets, purses, keys, scarves, and even a bike in the one-by-four-foot space! The fact that the bike folds helps a great deal, but a traditional bike could be mounted vertically on the wall to similar effect.

cozy kitchens
& dining rooms

I've seen many small kitchens that are used often—and are brimming with so many plates, pans, and cookbooks that they're nearly impossible to clean. I've also visited many small kitchens that are *never* used, sparse rooms in which the fridge contains only a few bottles of water, a condiment or two, and the occasional bottle of gift champagne. Neither is good.

Show me a kitchen that communicates the thoughts of a passionate chef (amateur, of course!) who knows where everything is and who can give you a stool and pull out a bottle of wine and pour you a glass—all while chopping up vegetables for the evening's dinner—and I'm in heaven. Show me this in a cozy, small kitchen and I'm in seventh heaven.

Some of the best restaurants in New York City have the smallest kitchens, and it doesn't stop them from producing amazing meals night after night. Even without a team of sous-chefs, you really don't need much space to have a great kitchen.

Ultimately, kitchens are for cooking, and the point of cooking is preparing good food and sharing it with others. And let's face it: Despite our most ambitious entertaining plans, most of us share our time in the kitchen with a very small number of people. The kitchens in this book are all small, too, but they are social centers and working kitchens just the same. Some of them incorporate a dining area, and some adjoin separate dining rooms, but all make ingenious use of the space they've got—and allow for entertaining, to boot. What's more, all of them are stylish in their own way.

GENERAL TIPS:

- ■ UNDER-COUNTER FRIDGES ROCK. The largest thing in any kitchen is a conventional fridge, and I firmly believe that we don't need all the space they afford. What most of us could use more of is counter space. Using an under-counter fridge (or two) can totally transform a small kitchen.

OVERLEAF Removing the interior walls and installing tall glass doors completely transformed the dark ground floor of this home. Inspired by 1970s design, the strong reds warm up the room further while radiant heating under the slate floors saves energy and eliminates the need for space-hogging radiators.

OPPOSITE This small kitchen demonstrates what can be done when the owners have enough of a budget to invest in some beautiful ingredients to open up the space. It is light and bright with warm, natural materials that please the eye, and has plenty of storage so they can keep it neat.

ABOVE In small homes, dining rooms are so near the kitchen that they double as prep space. This street find dining table was topped with a new piece of glass to allow for all occasions.

OPPOSITE Just off the kitchen, a collection of silver candlesticks brightens this dining table, which is also the owner's favorite place to work during the day.

- HANG THE GOOD STUFF. When storage is tight, hanging pots and pans from the ceiling can make a big difference and save a lot of space. But cheap pots and pans don't make the greatest statement. Use your small kitchen as an excuse to invest in a few better-quality pieces, and then hang them up and get excited about cooking more often.

- COOKTOPS SAVE SPACE. To further maximize counter space, opt for a cooktop and a wall oven, rather than a stand-alone stove. This allows you to unify the countertop and the cabinetry beneath, minimizing visual clutter and making use of a few more precious square inches.

- EXTEND THE KITCHEN. Everyone loves to hang out in the kitchen, but there's often not much room. Any sliver of space near your kitchen will suffice for a dining room as well as an alternate workspace for both cooking prep and other activities. Make sure your dining table is strong and practical for all of these activities, and keep it uncluttered so that it is always welcoming.

BLACK-AND-WHITE PREWAR UPDATE

Although the owners, Yiming Wang and her husband, Xian Zhang, both work in finance, their true passion is for design and photography. This artistic impulse was essential in planning the couple's kitchen renovation. The kitchen started out as a typical narrow galley, with the only entrance facing the front hall of the apartment. It had counters along both walls, and no room for any dining area at all—a vestige of an era when cooking was separated from dining. With a few simple, bold strokes, Yiming completely transformed the apartment, creating a more social kitchen area.

- LAYOUT—Opening up the kitchen to the main room with a new, much bigger doorway and breaking up the galley to create an open, elbow floor plan were the first (and most dramatic) moves in the renovation process.

ABOVE LEFT Floor-to-ceiling tiles are un-expected and exceedingly practical—like one giant, easy-to-clean backsplash. The cabinets, stovetop, faucet, and stainless-steel racks are all from IKEA. The marble floor tiles are from Home Depot and cost $3 each. The extra-thick white Carrera marble came from Chinatown in Brooklyn and was the cheapest option.

OPPOSITE Major floor-plan changes allowed for a much nicer cooking center and a small dining area, which makes use of the deep, table-height windowsills. An antique dining table adds that irregular, personal element that keeps a modern room from looking too much like one in a catalog.

OWNERS
Yiming Wang and Xian Zhang

PROFESSIONS
Financial analyst (Yiming);
Photographer (Xian)

LOCATION
Hell's Kitchen, New York City

TYPE
Studio, 500 square feet

■ STYLE—When I first saw this kitchen, I could have sworn the walls were painted black, and I loved the way they brought strong contrast to the shiny stainless-steel racks and made the countertop seem even whiter than it was. When I found out that the whole kitchen was tiled in black, I liked it even better—it was even more elegant than I'd first imagined, and much more durable, too. Wisdom has it correct that dark colors make spaces seem smaller, but in this case, the kitchen provides a delicious contrast to the all-white apartment. More than square footage, what we crave is variation between spaces—and this kitchen delivers.

OPPOSITE Playing on the power of contrast, the owner cut a hole in the wall, reconfigured the floor plan, and set her renovated kitchen apart from the rest of the white and wood–clad apartment with floor-to-ceiling glossy black tiles. Despite the dark color, plenty of light comes through the windows and gets bounced around by the reflective tiles. The end result is one of twinkling brightness, not gloom. In addition, the sun from the new doorway brightens the main room.

ABOVE Used sparingly, the color is all the more charming and eye-catching when it does appear.

■ TIP If you're designing a monochromatic room, add pops of a contrasting shade here and there to bring the palette to life.

THE FAMILY-FRIENDLY KITCHEN

Like many old city kitchens, this one was a small, narrow galley separated from the rest of the home. The owners, Brian Krex and Vanessa Ward, wanted to be able to cook, eat, and watch their kids playing all in one room. Removing a wall created an opening, but it took smart planning to maximize the space and create the impression that the wall had never been there at all. To pull off this feat, the couple enlisted the help of professional designers Anshu Bangia and William Agostinho. Brian and Vanessa were willing to tear everything out and start over from scratch. Their only requirement was the inclusion of a full-size, professional-quality stove for the passionate cook in the family.

ABOVE In addition to removing an intersecting wall, the designers stripped down some extra layers on the remaining kitchen walls, freeing up a few extra inches of floor and wall space. The materials they used for everything else—single sheets of zebrawood veneer for the upper cabinets, a one-and-a-quater-inch-thick slab of Calcutta Gold marble for the countertops—are luxurious and interesting and require no additional adornment. The durable stone floor tiles of the kitchen blend seamlessly with the rest of the apartment's dark wood flooring.

- LAYOUT—On approach, the focal point of the kitchen is the huge marble counter that stretches from the inner wall, where it serves as a work surface, all the way out into the family room, where it becomes, alternately, a bar for guests and a dinner table for the children. Similarly, the wainscoting wraps the space between the rooms. The chef's requested stove became the centerpiece of the room, while the slim Sub-Zero fridge was hidden around the corner out of sight.

- STYLE—The answer to maximizing this small space visually is white, white, and more white, with a dash of zebrawood, some stainless steel, and a dark floor for drama. The zebrawood cabinets command attention, but in doses that don't overwhelm. Instead, they seem to float on the wall and promote a light, airy feeling.

KEY INGREDIENTS
- Kitchen open to dining room
- Beautiful use of materials—marble and zebrawood
- Smart cabinetry

ABOVE This kitchen balances feminine, earthy details (like the sculptural vase on the wooden shelf) with harder, masculine materials like stainless steel.

ABOVE Concealing the microwave goes a long way toward improving the look of a kitchen.

■ TIP Extra outlets are always helpful, and any electrician should be able to wire an existing cabinet so that you don't even see the appliance's cords.

OPPOSITE, ABOVE, AND RIGHT
Plentiful cabinets provide storage, and specialized hinges and slides make the cabinets work even harder. A cabinet-mounted sliding garbage can is another instant upgrade toward a clutter-free kitchen, and sliding storage trays make it easier to access lesser-used cooking items. This is one of the advantages of spending more on your cabinets. For simple boxes with doors, go to IKEA, but if you want your trash to roll out, or your microwave and plates to slide away, a bigger investment is required.

OWNERS
Brian Krex and Vanessa Ward

PROFESSIONS
Freelance writer (Vanessa); Lawyer (Brian)

LOCATION
Upper West Side, New York City

TYPE
Two-bedroom, 1,630 square feet

THE SET DESIGNER'S ECO KITCHEN

It's not apparent at first glance, but one of the distinguishing features of this kitchen is its dedication to green design and reuse. Kelly Van Patter, a former television set designer and now an interior designer and the owner of a green housewares shop, has filled her home with pieces scavenged from shows she worked on, remnant materials she's creatively repurposed, and other easy-to-overlook items.

KEY INGREDIENTS
- Cut-down cabinet doors
- Dark floor, light walls
- Balanced layout

ABOVE Strong symmetry and a soothing, tonal color palette infuse this open-plan kitchen with ordered serenity. The counter is pieced together from remnant Venini marble, and the island is an IKEA butcher block that the owner had topped with stainless steel.

■ LAYOUT—During renovation, many of the walls that separated the kitchen were removed. Opening the kitchen up on every side made it bigger and sunnier, as light now passes across this central part of the home's ground floor. It also made a trio of rooms—kitchen, dining room, and office—one continuous work space, which Kelly often spreads out in when tackling large projects with a group of assistants.

■ STYLE—If light walls make a space feel larger, it also helps to have a dark floor. Sanded and stained, these original Douglas fir planks warm the room considerably and visually drop away, emphasizing the height of the ceiling; white-painted exposed beams allow the eye to travel up even farther. The owner used mostly soft, neutral colors as accents, to add variety to the white walls without disrupting the tone.

■ TIP When enlarging a kitchen by removing a wall, incorporating an island can help preserve the shape and enhance the practicality of the room.

OWNER
Kelly Van Patter

PROFESSION
Green interior and production designer

LOCATION
Highland Park, Los Angeles

TYPE
Two-bedroom, 1,500 square feet

THE SUNNY, RECYCLED KITCHEN

This joyful kitchen represents how completely you can transform a cramped, dark rental—even on a shoestring budget. Justina Blakeney is a writer and designer who started a successful company with her sister, making funky new clothing and housewares out of recycled materials and teaching others how to do the same. Upcycling, reusing, or recycling—whatever you want to call it—her eyes see possibility where others do not.

- STYLE—White paint is a tremendous ally when working with small spaces, but alone, it can mean a home that's bright but boring. The key is to add color to trim or accent walls and to hang or display items that are

ABOVE LEFT While everything in this kitchen is colorful, Justina has focused her palette on yellows and greens, which are easy to find in nature. Those two colors, along with the abundant Southern California sunlight from the two windows, transforms the galley kitchen into a cozy, cheerful space.

■ **TIP** Jot ingredients and instructions on the chalkboard before cooking, so you don't have to find a spot on the counter for the recipe book.

KEY INGREDIENTS

■ Fresh white paint with yellow and green trim

■ IKEA wood laminate flooring painted white

■ Round dining table made from recycled plates

ABOVE The original bones of this kitchen were nothing to write home about, and the best solution was to freshen them up (and disguise their flaws) with a few coats of bright white paint—often the only improvement a renter is allowed to make. To cover the old, dark linoleum floor that was sucking light from the apartment, the resident laid down affordable IKEA flooring and then painted it white. (Because the flooring has an artificial veneer, it won't hold the paint forever; still, it works as a short-term solution in a rental like this.) A rectangle of chalkboard paint provides cheap, changeable artwork that takes up zero space in a small kitchen.

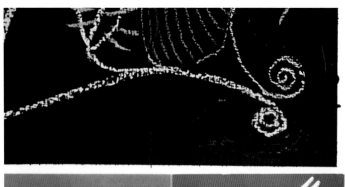

personal and original. Justina painted the ceiling molding and the cabinet doors bright yellow to perk up the space and attract the eye upward and around the room. Taking advantage of the one big wall, she also used chalkboard paint to make fun and changeable signage, while artwork, colorful plates, and fresh flowers give life and expression to the rest of the kitchen.

■ **TIP** I recommend using latex, water-based paints with "Low-VOC" or "Zero-VOC" on the label. These paints dry quickly, off-gas very little (or not at all), and are healthier for you and the air in your home (see Lists on page 293 for recommendations).

RENTER
Justina Blakeney

PROFESSION
Designer, author, and editor

LOCATION
Los Feliz, Los Angeles

TYPE
One-bedroom, 450 square feet

OPPOSITE Ever the recycler, Justina used photographs from an art exhibit's program to line the top edge of her tile backsplash. Easy to change when she tires of them, they add tons of personality to what could otherwise have been a much less inviting rental.

ABOVE Justina refinished the top of an unwanted table with a mosaic of broken china. She also capitalized on a shallow niche in the wall, making it the home for a hanging paper-towel dispenser she fashioned out of discarded wire and butcher's twine.

THE VERSAILLES KITCHEN

This apartment makes a strong first impression as being huge and white. The secret is that it's not very big at all—pale surfaces, lighting, and mirrors transform and enlarge the space. As the owner, Kelly Giesen, says, "Paint it and put a mirror behind it and it becomes something new."

- LAYOUT—After knocking down the wall to open up the galley kitchen to the main room, Kelly placed a dishwasher, a fridge, and a freezer under the countertop to preserve space. She also had her cabinets built sixteen inches deep, slightly deeper than is standard, so that she could fit all her dishware—and even her microwave—inside. The stove and sink were built into a marble-topped island that helps define the room and provides even more counter space.

KEY INGREDIENTS
- Mirrored surfaces
- White marble
- Under-counter appliances

OPPOSITE There's no room for clutter or messes in this gleaming-white kitchen. The bones of the room are completely new, as the original apartment was in very poor condition and not much was salvageable. Despite all the new construction, the owner has taken off the hard edge by adding timeworn elements wherever possible. In addition to purchasing vintage furniture and an old mirror and chandelier, she added antique glass to the cabinet doors and used glue-chip glass—an old-fashioned alternative to frosted glass—for the windowpanes.

LEFT To integrate the thirty-inch stainless steel Viking stove into the all-white kitchen, the marble countertop was cut to sheathe its edges.

- STYLE—Kelly's style is traditional and bright, but not fussy, and her desire for efficiency is positively modern. In the kitchen area, which is the darkest part of her house, her two ceiling fixtures are supplemented by under-counter lights that illuminate the marble work surface. (All the lights are even hooked up to remote-controlled dimmers!) Mirrors in the rear of the cabinets effectively multiply the sunlight from the other side of the room. The large slab of marble on the countertop and backsplash not only appears visually luxurious, but it also reflects tons of light and reduces visual clutter.

OWNER
Kelly Giesen

PROFESSION
Interior designer

LOCATION
Upper West Side, New York City

TYPE
One-bedroom, 725 square feet

RIGHT All the cabinets are backed with mirrors, which bounce even more light off the delicate dishware.

BELOW To maximize work surfaces (and make it easier to find food items), the owner installed Fisher & Paykel under-counter refrigerator drawers (and one freezer drawer) beneath her countertop.

ABOVE While most of the cabinet doors are fronted with antique glass to show off a collection of vintage stemware, the one that holds the microwave is fitted with custom-cut mirror panels that conceal the appliance and blend in seamlessly with the rest.

OPPOSITE You usually can't do too much to alter the shell of a rental apartment, but this one was in really bad shape. The solution? Covering every surface—including the floors—with fresh paint and color. Not content to simply set off the kitchen from the main room, the resident also used a subtle pairing of pale gray and white paint to add dimension to the kitchen's structural elements.

LEFT Flea-market coffee and sugar canisters play up the vintage look of the matching red-trimmed dishware set—which was actually bought new at a chain store.

KEY INGREDIENTS

- Strong white-and-blue color theme
- Open storage
- Generous lighting

THE UNDER-BED KITCHEN

Mat Sanders doesn't know who was responsible for building the loft over the kitchen in his postage-stamp-size studio, but it must have been done years ago. He inherited the apartment in 2004 from the previous tenant and quickly fell in love with it. Due to the apartment's prime location and the way it is set up perfectly for entertaining, Mat hosts more scheduled (and unscheduled) parties than many people with much bigger digs.

The secret to the tiny space's allure is the extremely high (eighteen-foot) ceiling, which allowed for the creation of an "upstairs" area for bed and storage, leaving nothing on the ground floor but the social area. The open, bar-style design of the kitchen, which functions dually as counter and dining table, is an inexpensive, remarkably compact, and intelligent solution that complements Mat's lifestyle.

- LAYOUT—The decision to have open shelving often can be a purely cosmetic one, but in this case, removing the kitchen cabinet doors

RENTER
Mat Sanders

PROFESSION
Actor and playwright

LOCATION
West Village, New York City

TYPE
Studio, 250 square feet

OPPOSITE Tucked under his loft bedroom, the resident's kitchen/dining nook combo makes the best use of limited space by connecting the kitchen to the small-scale living room, enlarging both at once.

ABOVE LEFT Magnetic spice containers, a no-fail space-saver, were never more useful than in this storage-starved kitchen.

ABOVE RIGHT Galvanized tins are a sensible way to corral typical pantry items, while concealing their labels. Mat tucks his less-attractive dishware and supplies behind a curtain on the back side of the bar. The striped curtain riffs on the apartment's nautical theme.

opened up the view and created additional visual square footage. Painted light blue, the cabinet backs recede, and the interiors feel airier.

■ STYLE—Two elements combine to render this kitchen bright and friendly. The first is contrast: This is the brightest area in a very dark room (the rest of the walls are painted navy blue, inspired, Mat says, by the feeling of standing on the deck of a ship at night). I often counsel people to paint their hallways dark when they want to make the adjacent rooms appear bigger.

The second factor at work is good lighting. Every room should have at least three sources, with plenty of distance between them, and this kitchen follows that rule. Two pendants illuminate the counter area, and a light over the stove makes for an attractive place to cook. Together, they drive the shadows out of the darkest part of the apartment, and beckon guests, appropriately, like lights on a ship.

KEY INGREDIENTS
- Mirrored wall with hidden doors
- White Corian counter and backsplash
- Baroque kitchen table and chairs

THE JEWEL-BOX KITCHEN

Gennadi Maryash and Terence Schroeder bought a small one-bedroom apartment on a perfectly unassuming Upper East Side block, gut-renovated it, and turned it into a study in contrasts. Rather than try to blend their opposing personal styles in such a compact space, each called dibs on one of the home's two common areas; now, a tiny, totally modern white kitchen nestles up against a baroque sitting room—walk from one room to the next and you feel as if you've landed on another planet. With the lion's share of the square footage going to the sitting room, the kitchen had to accomplish a lot in very little space.

- LAYOUT—Because the apartment's front door opens directly into the kitchen, this room is positioned as both the entrance and the central space around which all the others flow—making a well-planned configuration all the more important. Two of the walls serve as the primary storage areas for the whole apartment—one holds cooking supplies, the other, books. Clustering the storage areas and keeping the remaining walls free gives a much greater sense of space than spreading things out on each wall would.

- STYLE—The owners chose to make this room extremely modern, minimal, and as functional as possible. Since the pair does very little cooking (but throws lots of cocktail parties), they opted to devote only a small amount of space to a pair of burners and an under-counter dishwasher and refrigerator, and leave the bulk of the room free for socializing. They've been reported to fit as many as forty guests in the small home.

ABOVE Setting the sink into one continuous piece of Corian contributes to the streamlined, uncluttered look of the countertop.

OPPOSITE Swirls meet straight lines as a baroque sitting-room door opens into a modern kitchen. One of the most magical and exciting things about this space is the way the table and chairs create a dialogue between the minimal and decorative styles.

ABOVE LEFT This is the view through the front door. Aesthetics were important, so the cabinets were custom-built to fit the space, and the countertop and backsplash were done in durable, bright-white Corian—a worthy splurge. Like a hidden passageway, the bathroom door swings inward on the right, with only a sliver of a door handle to give it away.

LEFT Gennadi and Terence had uniform, minimal fronts made for their under-counter dishwasher and refrigerator, disguising the appliances completely (and cleverly). There's also a dish-washer hidden on the right side.

■ TIP Installing minimal cabinet and door pulls is a small change that can make a big difference in a room like this.

OWNERS
Gennadi Maryash and Terence
Schroeder

PROFESSIONS
Software engineer and
lecturer (Gennadi);
Architect (Terence)

LOCATION
Upper East Side, New York
City

TYPE
One-bedroom, 480 square feet

CENTER Bookshelves mounted near the front door keep on-the-go reading at the ready and provide a few options for stashing objects and mail as the owners enter.

ABOVE RIGHT This small kitchen contains the basic building blocks for enlarging any space. Keeping everything white and the floor space relatively empty were the first steps; the couple then loaded up two walls with storage and another with mirrored panels that added visual space where there was none.

Open storage at eye level and hidden storage below give the room a cleaner appearance than would floor-to-ceiling open shelving, which would be reflected and multiplied in the mirrored panes.

thoughts on small dining rooms

When I interview people and ask them what they'd like to do more of in their homes, they inevitably say, "Entertain." We all have a deep longing to share our homes, so it's important to create a place where we can sit down and enjoy a meal with friends or family. Even though it can be hard to carve out the space necessary for even the smallest dinner party, without a doubt, it can be done.

The dining rooms in this section are adjacent to kitchens, and because of space limitations, often are used as home offices as well. In every case, their owners have employed clever solutions that allow them to seat as many guests as possible without taking up too much space and have done so in a way that makes these areas not only functional additions to their homes but beautiful ones, too.

This dining room is situated in an open area between kitchen, hallway, and living room, but the colorful, oversize pendant lamp centers it and prevents it from being merely a transitional space. To conserve space, armless chairs can be pushed flush against the table's edge. With chalkboard paint from floor to ceiling, this deftly doubles as a meeting room.

OPPOSITE AND ABOVE This dining room is a favorite place to work, and the table is often covered with piles of drawings and notes. A modest but traditional space, the room is centered around a black dining set—purchased at IKEA, then painted—and the coordinating rug beneath it. The armless chairs have a very small footprint, and the table can be expanded with a leaf for more seating.

RIGHT This dining room makes extraordinary use of clear materials that nearly disappear before your eyes, making even a minuscule room feel vastly larger. Pale paint on the walls and floors contributes to the seamless, open feel.

OVERLEAF This dining room is in a very old apartment in Brooklyn that's divided into a number of tiny rooms. When the resident is not entertaining, she keeps her large dining table pushed against the wall, like a console; when company comes, she moves it to the center of the room, where it comfortably seats six.

■ **TIP** No room for one large table? Two consoles can also be pushed together to form one group-ready buffet.

OPPOSITE The box-like and modest dining room in this rental feels elegant because of the great furnishings that are centered on the window and pendant lamp. The horizontal shelf between the cabinets creates a long bar at the rear, the large mirror allows the eye to travel much farther, and the round dining room table softens the square room while also allowing easy passage from all sides.

ABOVE Fresh flowers and fruit are an easy and affordable way to warm up any room, and these, near Venice, California, are spectacular. Rich textures and organic materials like wood, flowers, and fruit attract the eye and bring the indoors to life.

thoughts on cabinet decor

Kitchens should feel warm—and cooking, conversation, and decor should all contribute to that effect. Reds, oranges, yellows, and even some greens are good candidates for kitchen color palettes. Brown, the most natural of colors, can serve as part of a warm mix. In most rooms, too much color will overwhelm the space, so my rule of thumb is to aim for 80 percent soft neutrals (including whites) and 20 percent bright colors. Kitchen cabinets can be a perfect vehicle for injecting color into a room, and they can also help define a space when it's open to a larger room.

Visiting so many small homes, I gradually came to realize that stainless steel, like white paint, can be used residentially to expand spaces. I found it everywhere, employed as an attractive, practical, and affordable alternative to stone, composite, or Corian. In addition, its light tone and shiny surface make it reflective and a good choice to brighten small, dark kitchens.

The photographs that follow show some great examples of colorful cabinets with different finishes that really bring these kitchens into focus.

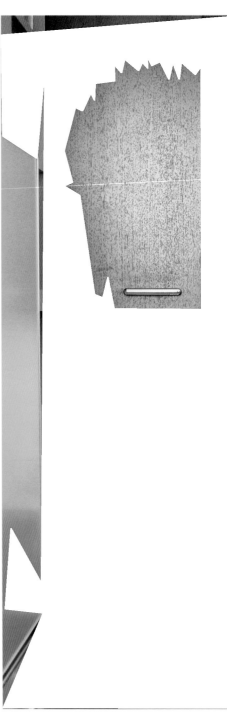

OVERLEAF, AND LEFT TO RIGHT These owners were inspired by the bright oranges and reds they saw in a kitchen design book from the 1970s, but they didn't want to turn their own kitchen into a replica of a fast-food restaurant. Using white on the walls and dark wood for the center cabinets and island allowed them to concentrate the strong colors in more digestible portions on either side of the room.

ABOVE AND LEFT Stainless-steel countertops are an especially good choice for homes with steel stoves and refrigerators, no matter what materials you use for the cabinet fronts. They create a continuous line that goes far to unify a room.

OPPOSITE The counters here are made of stainless steel wrapped around plywood and were meant to be temporary. The owners of this kitchen had planned to install stone countertops, but after living with the stainless, they loved its no-nonsense look and low maintenance so much that they canceled the stone and never looked back.

RIGHT This homeowner used bright orange cabinets to define the kitchen area, which isn't a room of its own. The empty white space above and on the sides balances the bright color in the middle—just the right amount of pop for the diminutive nook.

BELOW Rental apartments are notorious for the poor quality (and low style factor) of their kitchen cabinets, and in many cases, the renter's go-to solution for domestic eyesores—a few coats of paint—can make laminate look worse. Instead, this clever resident used two layers of Con-Tac paper (one in white, one in wood grain) and a stencil of a woodland scene to turn her kitchen's flaw into a focal point—and one that can be peeled off easily when it comes time to move out.

ABOVE In this open-plan kitchen, the cabinets have been shop sprayed deep tan with a very high gloss, which reflects a ton of the natural light that streams in from the adjacent room. This truly reads as one uniform accent wall.

BELOW One-piece sink/countertops are inexpensive and easy to keep clean and will never allow water to leak into your cabinets below, thanks to their lack of seams.

thoughts on open storage

Most restaurant kitchens use open storage exclusively, and I love homes that do, too. True, it can make a kitchen a little more visually busy, but I think it's a good type of busy—a signal that a kitchen is lively and has an aspiring chef in residence.

This type of solution works best when you've already pared down and are showcasing elements that you use often and that are of a high enough quality to be aesthetically attractive. That may mean you need to spend an afternoon transferring your sugar from the yellow box to a glass jar, replacing your cheap pots and pans with professional ones, or weeding out old and mismatched dishes from your collection, but once you've done it, you will have greatly enhanced your kitchen.

Restaurant-supply shops hold untold wonders for those in search of the most durable and functional kitchen items. This stainless-steel table provides both work surface and china storage and would also be a fitting island or bar in an open kitchen.

OPPOSITE IKEA Grundtal racks are used with S-hooks to hold pots and pans in the otherwise unused space above the kitchen sink.

ABOVE, LEFT TO RIGHT Stainless-steel towel bars are a creative way to store and display the latest cooking publications.

The stainless-steel picture rails in this kitchen echo the shiny surfaces of the appliances while encouraging the owners to flip through cooking magazines and books and try out new recipes for the evening meal. What's more, the picture rails take up almost no space, and the volumes displayed double as artwork.

RIGHT A skilled small-space dweller takes advantage of every conceivable storage opportunity. Here, a narrow nook becomes a perfect makeshift pantry with the addition of a few stained particle-board shelves.

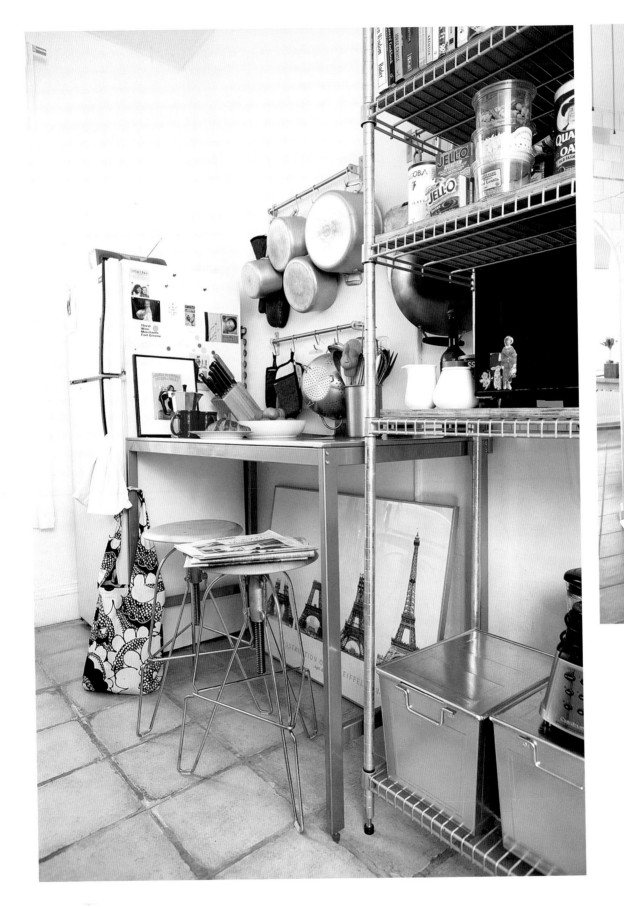

OPPOSITE Metro shelving is another great workhorse for open storage: Originally created for commercial purposes, its clean design and shiny surfaces make it incredibly space efficient and visually attractive, and the shelves are fully adjustable. The only drawback is that its contents must be vertically organized!

ABOVE The tiled walls of this sweet kitchen meant that the residents couldn't add a shelf or a rack on the wall by the stove. Hanging one from the ceiling solved the problem, while emphasizing the generous height of the ceiling.

ABOVE This ceiling-mounted pot rack, suspended over a kitchen island, transformed the space, giving focus to the kitchen and separating it from the dining area right next to it—not to mention freeing up a hefty portion of cupboard storage.

TOP When Sara Kate and I spotted this incredibly space-conscious vertical wine rack in a restaurant one evening, we knew we had to get one for ourselves. While rare and precious vintages should be stored under climate- and light-controlled conditions, this type of storage is perfectly fine for the table wines we drink and replace regularly.

compact
living rooms

OVERLEAF The deep pink of the nearly wall-to-wall area rug calls out the smattering of bright colors elsewhere in the room—but does so in a quiet way. The sheepskin rugs on top of it add even more softness, while breaking up the expanse of the strong hue. Because our windows are not particularly pretty, with their black aluminum frames, I hung long, sheer linen curtains to soften the harsh edges and lead the eye from the floor up over the top of the window. Remember: Long curtains make for tall walls, and short curtains make for shorter walls.

ABOVE From this angle, this room feels wonderfully white and open. The curtain (which surrounds the bedroom) and the wall of windows visually balance out the opposite wall of storage. Illuminating the shelves is a long line of track lighting, which serves to further expand the space. Track fixtures illuminate a room without taking up any floor space—and they are so much less obtrusive than they used to be!

ABOVE RIGHT Chandeliers with many glass pieces are old-fashioned but were designed intentionally to amplify light so that rooms would be better illuminated and feel more spacious. They still work this way, and they couldn't be more hip.

In most homes in the United States, the living room is the biggest room—with lots of space for furniture and plenty of large-scale options available. It's all too easy to find the generous leather sectional sofa, the overstuffed La-Z-Boy, and the wide-screen television with surround sound—and all too difficult to find solutions when you don't have that much space. In fact, it's only in the past five years that major manufacturers have taken any notice of those of us with smaller needs.

The living rooms in this chapter are compact, but they are also inviting social centers. None of them is conventional, and all of their owners worked to solve problems such as funky floor plans and to give the space multiple options. One living room doubles as an office and a bedroom, one is engulfed by electrical boxes, and one is at the top of such a tight staircase that only a daybed could fit through the corridor. Despite all this, every one of them is a place where the residents can let their hair down and relax—exactly what a living room should be.

GENERAL TIPS

- FIRST, GET THE RIGHT SIZE SOFA. The biggest—and usually the most expensive—piece of furniture in any living room is the sofa. The whole room depends on it, so when planning your space, start by making sure you choose a sofa that is the right size, that fits through your door, and

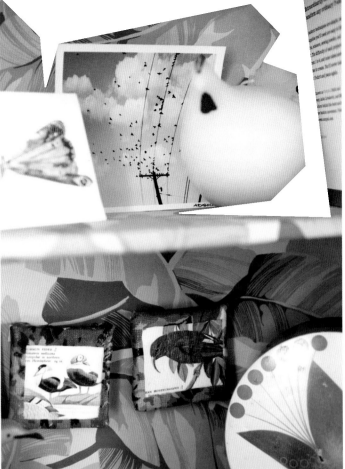

that you love. For small spaces, I recommend getting a model that will allow for enough room to fit side tables and lamps on either side, and space to walk around it—about two feet of clearance on either end. Look for sofas that are raised off the ground on exposed legs and sofas without arms; both preserve a room's flow and make the room feel larger and more open.

- ▪ DON'T FOCUS ON THE TV. Remember that living rooms should be social centers, designed for relaxing with friends first, and watching television second—a rule that holds true even if you live alone. Living rooms organized exclusively around the television are energy and conversation killers. To counteract the "movie theater" tendency that is all too common in today's homes, equip your living room with at least three seating positions that all face one another, making a sort of semicircle around the center of your room. One of these can be a sofa, but you still need two more.

- ▪ STOCK UP ON OTTOMANS, CUBES, OR POUFS. When space is really short, ottomans or other shapes such as cubes or poufs are incredibly useful for providing flexible extra seating, and many can double as side tables, footrests, and in the case of those with removable tops, discreet storage spaces.

Justina Blakeney's living room is a riot of color and filled with belongings that delight the eye. She uses every possible space to not only display her collections of artwork and jewelry, but also to hide the aging bones of her rental bungalow. Of particular note is the vintage vinyl wallpaper that came from the walls of a hotel in Disneyland.

KEY INGREDIENTS
- Armless daybed
- Large, colorful rug
- Light walls

THE DAYBED LIVING ROOM

Our own living room faces a number of limitations: very tight space, low ceilings, and a fourth-floor location that can be reached only via a narrow staircase. What it does have going for it are great light and the fact that, structurally, it is in fantastic condition.

- LAYOUT—The rug was the first thing we purchased, and I chose it because it was large enough to go nearly wall to wall, providing a perimeter to the sitting area. Even though the room was little, and I knew we'd need small furniture, I still wanted it to feel luxurious and big somewhere!

    For a sofa, we chose a daybed—not only because it was the only thing we could fit up our staircase and through our doorway, but also because,

ABOVE Although the colors in the throw pillows are bold, their patterns incorporate the neutral tones seen throughout the room, so they seem like a part of the plan and not a last-minute addition.

OPPOSITE Low sofas call for low side tables. We've avoided bringing in a coffee table so far, and use only a few little stools for side tables so as not to clutter the space.

- TIP Cutting stools like this one from Ikea down to the exact size you want is a cheap, easy solution that can save you a lot of time trolling through shops.

since it lacks bulky arms, it was our only hope of adding a spare bed while keeping a sense of spaciousness. Two round bolsters serve as a backrest (you can see them tucked behind the throw pillows on page 101).

■ STYLE—The first thing I do when dealing with a small space like this one is paint the ceiling bright white, the trim a softer white (Benjamin Moore's White Dove), and the walls a shade of white with even more color in it (Benjamin Moore's China White). This keeps the reflective light as high as possible, and the layering of colors adds some subtlety. A darker floor, either covered with a rug or stained, provides a nice, warm anchor for the room and falls away visually, while white walls draw the eye upward. These two tricks alone can really transform a space.

■ TIP Take your time when choosing furniture. It allows you to figure out what you really need—and to realize it's a lot less than you think.

OPPOSITE A long, slim bookcase (repurposed from Sara's father's law office) houses our books and stereo system without eating up much floor space—and doubles as a side table for the upholstered rocking chair (originally a nursing chair). To make the most of the space, we furnished it slowly, adding only pieces that were perfect and that we'd want to have with us for a long time.

ABOVE When favorite, well-used items are beautiful, like these knitting supplies, they don't always have to be hidden away between uses.

RENTERS
Sara Kate and Maxwell Gillingham-Ryan

PROFESSIONS
Food writer (Sara Kate); Interior designer (Maxwell)

LOCATION
West Village, New York City

TYPE
Two-bedroom, 725 square feet

THE COLLECTOR'S LIVING ROOM

What is most interesting about this room is that it breaks nearly all the "rules" for making small spaces seem bigger—it's painted dark and filled with objects—but it still feels expansive. One of Michelle McCormick's secrets is that she's incorporated many containers, all of which house smaller collections. Everything is functional, and even the bookcases, which are made of old wooden boxes, are attractive objects in their own right.

- LAYOUT—For many people—particularly small-space dwellers—the first instinct is to push the sofa up against a wall when arranging a living room. Although that move would have created a larger sitting area here, positioning the couch a few feet away from the wall allowed a long run of storage and a nice flowing pathway, with access to the room's windows. The more places to roam, the bigger a room feels.

KEY INGREDIENTS
- Tall walls with white trim and ceiling
- Pale, slim-legged furniture
- Storage as sculpture

ABOVE Very little in this room is newly purchased; most is vintage, found on the street or bought at flea markets, antiques shops, and garage sales. Everything, however, is in great shape: The sofa and chair were newly upholstered in gray Larsen fabric, the prints and pictures have been lovingly framed, and the lamps have all been rewired. Age may give the room beauty, but it is this attention to renewal that makes it comfortable and fresh.

PRECEDING PAGE All along the back wall, wooden boxes in all shapes and sizes, clamped together with antique vises, store and display a tremendous amount of the owners' belongings in one place. The solution is highly adaptable: The shape can be changed, more crates can be added, and the crates can all turn into handy moving containers when the time comes to relocate.

RIGHT Vise clamps hold these boxes together. Wood screws or glue would provide a more permanent fix.

■ TIP Ask your local wine store to save any wooden crates they plan on throwing out, and stack them together on the floor. Secure higher boxes to the wall with picture wire instead of clamps.

OPPOSITE Michelle's collection of antique lighting and mirrored objects is all the more striking against the dark blue-green of the walls.

RENTERS
Michelle and Tracy McCormick

PROFESSIONS
Design director (Michelle); Senior project manager (Tracy)

LOCATION
Wilshire Boulevard, Los Angeles

TYPE
One-bedroom, 875 square feet

■ STYLE—The residents have also used a lot of vertical elements to draw the eye upward and away from the density of the sitting area. Note how the framed artwork climbs up and over the top of the wall like a cloud drifting across a deep blue sky. If the ceiling had not been so high, it would have been hard to get away with these intense colors and the abundance of stuff.

RENTERS
Timothy and Laura Dahl

PROFESSIONS
Entrepreneur and blogger
(Timothy); Fashion designer
(Laura)

LOCATION
Santa Monica, Los Angeles

TYPE
One-bedroom, 900 square
feet

KEY INGREDIENTS
- Large, bold rug
- Rotating chair and ottoman
- Slim, light sofa

THE SATELLITE LIVING ROOM

Laura and Timothy Dahl recently moved from New York to Los Angeles and found a home with so much more space than their last one that they actually needed to buy additional furniture. But along with the increase in square footage, they inherited a new problem: The central room of the small bungalow was bisected by a hallway, which made it difficult to design one cohesive living room. Their solution was to position the main living room on the larger, more beautiful side of the space, under the big picture window, and to create a secondary sitting area on the other side of the room, which could easily be integrated with the main area as needed.

- LAYOUT—This living room is flexible. The side chair, pillows, and ottoman are easily moved to accommodate more or fewer people, while the large rug—an element second in importance only to the sofa—helps to center the living area. Because it fills the space entirely, rather than stopping at

ABOVE Small mirror details on the table in front of the larger mirror magnify the sparkle.

OPPOSITE With its own chair, side table, rug, and lamp, this area has all it needs to be a stand-alone nook for reading or sipping a cup of coffee. While small objects may fit better into smaller rooms, adding the occasional large-scale object (like this mirror) creates drama and enhances the sense of space.

With its slim, low-rise arms and legs that allow a view of the space underneath, the sofa helps enlarge the space and lighten it visually. Paring down is still the best way to make the most of a small space, and this living room contains nothing but the essentials.

ABOVE The view out Timothy and Laura's picture window echoes the artwork on the adjacent wall, and they treat it like the focal point that it is, leaving it free of blinds or curtains and relying on the trees in the yard to give them privacy.

RIGHT Clear and white *objets* atop the fireplace (across the room from the sofa) add a touch of whimsy without screaming for attention.

the sofa's legs, the bold rug gives the grouping more presence.

- ■ STYLE—There are three big things in this room that vary the scale and give it impact, helping to distract from the very plain Sheetrock walls: the tall trio of lights, the floor mirror, and the large piece of art behind the sofa. Each of these leads your eye from the floor up to the ceiling and draws attention to the height of the walls, making them seem a lot grander than they are.

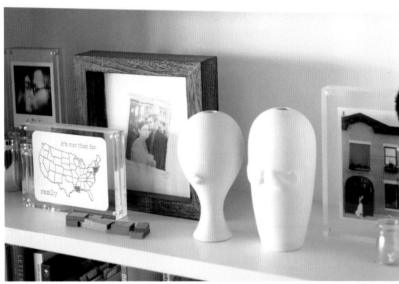

THE EVERYTHING-WALL LIVING ROOM

When the owners, Vané and Chad Broussard, bought this studio apartment in 2004, it was as much space as they could afford, and they knew they had to use every inch of it. They both wanted to be able to work from home, entertain friends, and store the tools of their active lives, such as his racing bike and her sewing station. Luckily, they are both designers, so figuring out how to maximize the space with style came naturally for them.

- LAYOUT—We can all live with a certain amount of visual clutter, but not if it's all around us. The secret to this room is that all the storage has been condensed to one wall on the side of the apartment. Built-ins are the best way to centralize storage and use every inch of wall space. There are no shadows or gaps, and they don't lose their plumb vertical lines the way standing bookshelves do.

KEY INGREDIENTS

- Custom wall storage
- Curtain to hide bedroom
- Track lighting

OPPOSITE Family photos command the eye-level shelves of the multitasking built-ins.

■ TIP Due to their size, sofas can be useful in creating "walls" and definition between rooms where there is none.

ABOVE In the owners' living room, custom built-ins hold clothing, a television and a stereo, the couple's books, and even a small office. A large green rug is used to center the space, and the sofa blocks off the bedroom area and faces the social area away from it (adding some privacy to the alcove).

OWNERS
Vané and Chad Broussard

PROFESSIONS
Interior designer and blogger
(Vané); Architectural designer
(Chad)

LOCATION
Brooklyn Heights, New York

TYPE
Studio, 500 square feet

■ STYLE—The owners really like the look of white lacquer furniture with walnut veneers, so they integrated these elements in their storage wall. The walnut warms the room and adds a rich organic texture, but there's not so much of it that it darkens the room. This room follows the 80/20 rule and feels balanced; the strong colors are no more than 20 percent of the entire color palette.

ABOVE Using all the available space, a pair of stacked closet bars maximizes the capacity of this concealed wardrobe and provides no hint of clothes in the living room.

RIGHT These small beauties lend some variety to the shelves, which neatly arrange books, binders, magazines, and files. Shelves that are just for storage can be oppressive, but these are delightful.

■ TIP Adding different shapes and textures to a bookshelf breaks up the monotony of straight vertical and horizontal lines.

OPPOSITE Chad's compact, ultra-efficient mini office provides a place for everything and doesn't waste an inch in the process. While the file cabinet is typically the least attractive thing in an office, this modern, streamlined one blends well with the white shelving around it. The overhead shelf's fabulous built-in dividers allow the owners to slot in magazines, books, or even papers without putting them in containers first.

THE INDUSTRIAL LIVING ROOM

This room is in the center of the most challenging home I visited. A stone's throw from the Williamsburg Bridge, it used to be a grimy, cavelike space before anyone moved in. Now, thanks to David Alhadeff's creative eye, it is a sun-filled retreat that feels lovable and charming.

- LAYOUT—There is enough room here to place seating on all sides of the coffee table, but the owner has chosen to break up the seating, using two sofas, a chair, and cushions. The space is welcoming and completely focused on the social circle—not on the television, which sits off to the side.

OPPOSITE Fresh paint can work wonders. What could have been an eyesore—a tangle of electrical boxes and wires—has been painted and integrated into a display of art.

ABOVE Much of the color is positioned on or near the ground, creating the overall effect of tall walls and a much larger room. A big galvanized tub by the sofa holds more than a year's worth of magazines. It's hard to get to those on the bottom, but this organic pile of glossies looks powerfully compelling.

■ **TIP** If your space is small, or if you've got a lot that you want to fit into a room, make sure there is some way for the eye to keep flowing so that it can rest after taking in a lot of dense objects.

■ STYLE—This room's strength is the balance between the white, open space and the crowded, dense, colorful patterns that fill the sofa and cover the floor. The viewer's eye goes right to the yummy pillows on the sofa, then up the quiet walls, and finally back to the rug and pillows in the foreground before starting all over again. This is an example of good visual flow.

OWNER
David Alhadeff

PROFESSION
Modern design store owner

LOCATION
Williamsburg, Brooklyn

TYPE
Two-bedroom, 1,200 square feet

OPPOSITE The apartment had no shelving of any kind, so David used a cutout in the wall to mount glass shelves that exactly fill the space. Perched on ordinary hardware-store brackets, the glass plank shelves take up much less visual space. To the left, a panel of backlit Plexiglas gives the room a warm, ambient glow at night.

ABOVE Funky pillows on the floor are not only stylish, they eliminate the need for additional chairs.

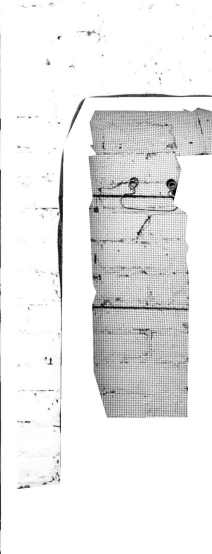

THE MULTILAYERED LIVING ROOM

This room is a model for those who wish to be highly decorative in a small space. In a humble Hell's Kitchen walk-up with very little space, the owner, Luis Caicedo, has created a sparkling, luxurious oasis with tons of unique decorative objects from his travels. It's a lot to take in at first, but his skill at arranging ties everything together.

■ LAYOUT—Despite the lack of square footage, the ceilings and windows in this room are lovely and tall, which makes them perfect elements to

ABOVE LEFT This room is far from spare, but the mostly neutral palette and the careful furniture arrangement prevent it from feeling overwhelming.

ABOVE The apartment's nonfunctioning fireplace has been transformed into an artistic display with ambient light.

RIGHT Tucked in a window niche, this antique chair can be pulled into action in the main area when extra guests arrive. The owner kept the apartment's original wood floors and painted them black. He also left the old, chipped-paint radiators in place as is, and their obvious age plays well with his decorative antiques.

accentuate. Luis uses a very formal, centered arrangement to allow for as much flow as possible around the perimeter of the room. The decor draws the eye upward from the strong border of the white rug to the sofa, and up the tall curtains to the ceiling, from which a Nelson pendant lamp hangs.

■ STYLE—Luis used primarily neutral colors and whites along with reflective surfaces to pull in as much sunlight as possible from the two windows and reflect it around the room. All the furniture, like the lacquer sideboard and the Lucite coffee table, is raised up off the floor on legs, creating a lighter visual feeling.

MATTHEW BARNEY
THE CREMASTER CYCLE

TOM OF FINLAND
THE ART OF PLEASURE

Once a wall sconce from an Art Deco
theater, this antique head now serves
as a lamp. The gold-leaf bowl to the
right is Luis's own design.

Excellent use of metallic accents and light furnishings keeps the room bright. The curtains, which function as vertical pillars, can be clearly seen here as they solidly frame the windows.

OWNER
Luis Caicedo

PROFESSION
Interior and product designer

LOCATION
Hell's Kitchen, New York City

TYPE
Railroad studio, 400 square feet

thoughts on bookshelves

I love shelves filled with books, art, and personal collections, but they have to be beautifully arranged. You can store a lot in plain sight, and if well executed, the display will add beauty to your home rather than contracting your space with clutter. In fact, I'd rather see people not hide so much storage, because bad things happen behind closed doors, and messes get messier and more difficult to deal with when you don't see them. Here are my rules of thumb:

- Keep storage out in the open, and keep it neat.

- Cluster the items in your open storage for visual impact.

- Store larger, heavier items closer to the ground (and small things on top).

- Decrease the height between shelves as you go up, for visual balance.

- Use shelving when you need an office. Small offices easily can be fit into bookshelves by installing a wider surface at desk height.

Integrating a small office into a wall of shelves doesn't take up much more space than shelves alone and affords a dramatic increase in efficiency.

This is a great example of cluster storage: Putting everything in one place creates a nice visual impact and leaves the rest of the home more streamlined. The open wall space on either side also helps maintain a sense of balance.

OPPOSITE For the most minimal effect, the whiteness of this slim modern shelving reduces its visual impact.

ABOVE AND RIGHT These shelves have a very light, open design and are easily installed, expanded, and removed without any damage to the walls. This type of shelving is a favorite for the way it shows off books and objects, but it requires careful tending so that it doesn't become too messy.

thoughts on televisions and stereos

Televisions shouldn't dominate the living room, but they should be easy to watch, so the design elements surrounding the television (or the stereo system) require thoughtful treatment. Here are some rules of thumb for making electronics more eye-catching—in a good way:

- Keep televisions slim.

- Keep audio components small.

- Opt for silver-framed televisions when possible. They are visually lighter.

- Take extra time to hide as much of the wiring as possible.

- Keep large televisions low so they don't overwhelm the room.

This low-profile solution places the screen at a nice viewing height for when you're sitting. (People generally mount their TVs too high, which calls more attention to them.)

■ **TIP** Don't have a spare fireplace in your home? Surprise—this homeowner didn't either. She simply mounted an antique fireplace mantel on the wall and tucked her set inside.

ABOVE, LEFT TO RIGHT This genius
storage idea was built by the homeowner
himself: a drawer that opens upward
instead of sideways.

OPPOSITE A wonderful, utterly unique solution, mounting this flat-screen monitor on an old painter's easel gives it a much less high-tech feeling, and takes attention away from its large size.

ABOVE Here's another solution that is about as spartan and as small as you get: In our home, we don't have a television or a stereo—all we have are our computers, our iPods, and this Apple hi-fi unit, which provides plenty of sound for our small apartment. We view movies, listen to music, and even watch big events like the inauguration with this setup, because so much of it is streamed live on the Web now. The computers can be put away when we're not using them, and the speaker has a very small footprint on our bookcase/sideboard.

RIGHT If hiding the television isn't a priority (or an option), it still pays off visually to keep the cords and cables out of sight. A professional installer can snake the wires through the wall and give the device the same clean outline as a hanging work of art. Here, a wall color in a similar shade to the television's frame helps it blend in even more.

miniature
bedrooms

OPPOSITE With a loft this high, a world of possibilities opens up: Here, track lighting and ceiling-mounted curtains maximize every last inch of vertical space. And because the curtains extend all the way to the ceiling, they effectively function as a bedroom wall, allowing one person to sleep while the other stays up in the living room.

ABOVE LEFT This bedside table is filled, but beautifully so. If you love to collect, it's important to work your pieces into your home, not hide them in a closet.

ABOVE RIGHT This wood-carved Buddha is a reminder that the bedroom is the most private and sacred space in a small home, and an apt place for special objects like this. Keeping the bedroom calm and uncluttered is paramount.

When you're a child, your bedroom is the center of your world; it's your fort, your place to dream at night. As you get older, it can lose its hold on your imagination and become simply the place where you sleep, set up your computer, and store too many winter clothes, or, occasionally, park an exercise bike. It can also lose its romantic potential.

A bedroom doesn't need to be big to allow for a good night's sleep, and working with a smaller space lets people get creative and put the excitement back in, because there's nothing more inviting than a cozy, snug space. Thomas Jefferson designed a bed in Monticello for his daughter that was like a cabinet, hidden between two walls, and the following chapter reveals the creativity of a modern-day couple who located a bed near the ceiling that can be surrounded by soft blackout curtains so it feels like it's in a treetop. There are also beds built on lofts, beds tucked in small rooms, beds in living rooms, a bed in an office, and a very empty bedroom that looks huge only because there's nothing in it.

My general advice is that bedrooms should be calm, uncluttered, and very clean—and if at all possible, nothing should be stored under the bed, as this sort of clutter can detract from restful energy. In a small space, avoiding under-bed storage can be difficult; nonetheless, it helps to try to

keep things as pared down and neat as you can. Here are a few other tips for making a small bedroom better.

- USE AN ACCENT WALL TO BRIGHTEN THE ROOM. Lighter colors will expand your walls, but they can be boring. Painting one wall darker—usually the one behind the head of your bed—will give you plenty of color, anchor the bed, and allow the other walls to seem even lighter and more expansive.

- BUILD UPWARD TO FIND MORE ROOM. We generally like being off the ground and raised up in the air a bit (even very low bedrooms in Asian cultures set beds on raised floors). Remember wanting to sleep in the top bunk? If square footage is really tight, building a loft bed can double your space and make your bedroom even more private than it was before.

- INSTALL PLENTY OF LIGHT. Even if you're not a fan of reading in bed, having lots of lights that are easy to turn on will make your bedroom seem bigger and more luxurious. Shadows make spaces feel small, so be sure to have a light on either side of your bed and at least one additional lamp at the entrance.

ABOVE LEFT Books and vintage cameras on display in this bedroom become conversation pieces.

ABOVE RIGHT The bookcase was originally an upright case that was turned on its side and legs were attached. Storage can be turned into decor when edited and assembled with care.

OPPOSITE Off to the side of this bedroom, there is a surprise: a closet that has been emptied and turned into a meditation space with a stunning slate accent wall. Closets can be used in unexpected ways to add a new sense of space and possibility to small homes with a limited number of rooms.

THE ELEVATED CUBE BEDROOM

Hilary Padget and Anthony Harrington, both architects, built this amazing bedroom structure in their rental apartment, which went on to win our Apartment Therapy Smallest Coolest Home Contest in 2008.

Inspired by the work of Japanese architect Shigeru Ban, the structure was conceived as a composite of many pieces of furniture that coordinate to create a small house. With a bedroom on top, which locks it all together, an office inside, and an entertainment center on the outside, the structure miraculously creates three discrete rooms out of one big one.

- LAYOUT—As with other loft bedrooms, the first concern here was to locate the bedroom area as deeply inside the apartment as possible to afford privacy and maintain a large, communal space by the window. Centered opposite the windows and the living room, the large structure

LEFT Loft bed owners often suffer for lack of privacy, but here full, light-blocking curtains mounted on a smooth track allow one person to stay up working in the main room, while the other gets a secluded rest up top.

OPPOSITE A view through one of the two entrances beneath the platform reveals that raising the bedroom allowed for more closet space than most apartments twice this size might have. Everything here was designed to be portable and as green as possible. Unlike many built-in structures, this can be easily taken apart and moved, since the furniture-grade Baltic birch plywood sheets fit together without fasteners.

creates two natural hallways, one leading to the front door and the other leading to the bathroom (on the right). This flow around three sides provides visual breathing room and easy access.

■ STYLE—A dominant structure like this required some style tweaks so that it didn't take up too much visual space and overwhelm the room. White paint and generous lighting make the surrounding space seem expansive and bright, and the light plywood, textiles, and white ceiling fan further blend in.

The form of this bedroom structure is so strong that Hilary and Anthony barely had to decorate, but imagine what they could do if they decided to paint the pieces white and experiment with a soft color on the walls; imagine stained, dark floors and a big chandelier over the living room; imagine curtains that didn't stop at the bed but went all the way down to the floor on all sides.

RENTERS
Hilary Padget and Anthony Harrington

PROFESSIONS
Architects

LOCATION
Fort Greene, Brooklyn

TYPE
Studio, 460 square feet

OPPOSITE Viewed from the opposite direction, the inside of the structure shows another bonus of building vertically: a small, streamlined home office. This one has its own overhead lighting in addition to the task lamp, and windows to the rest of the apartment let in natural light.

BELOW In this compact, low-rise bedroom, every surface opens to reveal more storage. Cabinets behind the bed hold all the extra linens, as well as reading material and alarm clocks.

THE DIVIDER BOOKSHELF BEDROOM

Studio residents are faced with the formidable challenge of fitting a bed-room into a wide-open living room. While the first inclination is usually to put the bed as far away from the door as possible so that guests don't have to walk around it, placing it in front of the window may result in a lack of privacy, and sectioning it off with a wall could keep all the light from getting to the rest of your home. This bedroom avoids these pitfalls. Using a translucent shelving system as a divider, owner Noah Posnick was able to build up a wall that both provides privacy and allows tons of light to pass through.

■ LAYOUT—When deciding where to position his Cubitec divider, Noah factored in not just the size of his bed, but also the pair of side tables he wanted to complement it. There's plenty of room for getting around the bed, and also plenty of privacy, as the head of the bed is far away from the entrance.

KEY INGREDIENTS
■ Cubitec shelving divider
■ Custom-made Parsons table
■ Solar and blackout shades

ABOVE A uniform, white (and clear) palette helps the furniture disappear behind the translucent shelving. Adding a piece of artwork to the back of the unit makes this feel more like a real room, not just a hidden space.

OWNER
Noah Posnick

PROFESSION
Commercial director

LOCATION
Greenwich Village, New York
City

TYPE
Studio, 537 square feet

■ STYLE—Noah has injected warm colors into his home though his furnishings and artwork. Note the brown curtains, desk, sofa, and large painting with dashes of red. In the bedroom, the primary objective was light reflection. Translucent furniture and accessories like the glass lamps and the Cubitec side tables both contribute to that goal, and almost disappear visually.

ABOVE LEFT A few silver highlights give the all-white room the sparkle it needs to avoid being bland.

ABOVE RIGHT Blackout curtains make it possible to position the bedroom so near to the apartment's expansive windows. Because Noah also has his office by the bed, he installed two types of shading on the large windows: blackout curtains for sleeping, and solar shades to filter the bright sunlight during the daytime.

While most of the cubes in the room-dividing shelving system have view-obscuring frosted back panels, those at eye level have been left open so that the owner can see out. While it's generally not a good thing to put one's office in the bedroom because it can bring daily stress into the room, here it works nicely. The desk, which is wide and thin, provides an uncluttered, balancing element to the bed and doesn't seem "officey."

THE MINIMAL BEDROOM

Simple and uncluttered, this lovely room radiates light and openness and is the perfect antidote to any stressful, busy, and overstimulating day. One of the secrets to the spaciousness of this room is, of course, that there's not much in it, but the reason it's attractive has to do with the great care the owners, Tina and Gary Eisenberg, have taken to include a few perfect pieces.

- LAYOUT—The first thing that makes the queen-size bed feel broad and expansive is its low, wide frame and mattress (no box spring), which sit centered on the room's longest wall, flanked by bedside tables and lamps. ■ TIP Centering furniture contributes to a restful, grounded, and calming feeling.

- STYLE—A sparse room can be boring, but this one isn't. The uninterrupted blue accent wall behind the bed becomes a sky above the brown wood floor, and the surprisingly tall toy giraffe seems to be walking through it. Shifts in scale also feature strongly here, from the giraffe and the large French poster to the small bonsai tree and the red tricycle.

ABOVE LEFT This room offers so little visual stimulation that what *is* there gains full attention: a nature-themed photograph by Myoung Ho Lee, the simple shapes of the reclaimed-lumber side tables, and the glossy-white rounded top of the bedside lamp.

ABOVE This shapely white rug's rounded edge contrasts nicely with the straight lines of the wall and the bed, and against a sky-blue backdrop, it evokes dreamy clouds.

OPPOSITE Vintage accessories, like the child's tricycle and the French bicycle poster, balance the modern, somewhat stark lines of a new-construction apartment.

les nouveaux
101-102
PEUGEOT

un nouveau style de v

OWNERS
Tina Roth Eisenberg and
Gary Eisenberg

PROFESSIONS
Graphic designer and blogger
(Tina); Kitchen designer (Gary)

LOCATION
Downtown Brooklyn,
New York

TYPE
Two-bedroom, 1,185 square
feet

THE FOUR-POSTER BEDROOM

To get to this tiny bedroom, interior designer Jen Chu has to walk through a closet, then slip sideways into the space, which is just large enough to fit a full-size mattress. Once she is inside, however, the beautiful and light-filled room feels like a little oasis within the busy city.

Jen's inspired idea here was to take something that is typically large—a four-poster bed—and fit it into a very small space, in order to make the bedroom feel grand. She's living proof that you don't have to be a minimalist to maximize the feeling of your bedroom.

■ LAYOUT—Since the mattress fills this room, everything is oriented vertically: the bed is raised up to allow for storage underneath, and shelves line one wall all the way to the ceiling. At night, for sleeping, the head of the bed is toward the window, but during the daytime, the bed is made up like a daybed in the other direction with a long headboard on the left wall. This crucial design detail makes the bed seem grander, keeps

ABOVE The chandelier, which adds old-fashioned elegance to the room, was a lucky find at the Brooklyn Flea Market. Its large scale is surprising, but the crystals reflect so much light that it adds more than it takes away.

More than being the major
statement piece in the room, this
four-poster platform bed is also the
workhorse, hiding suitcases, off-season
clothing, and even an air conditioner in
its depths. A bedroom like this isn't
found, but made. Starting with simple
cinder blocks and a metal grate, the
resident created a bed frame, plopped
the mattress down on top of it, and
attached the four posts and their top rail
to the floor and the ceiling. She then
mounted long shelves to the wall and
attached them to the posts so that they
would be sturdy enough to carry plenty
of weight. With a little TLC, even the
humblest of materials can look like
design pieces. Here, plain wood planks
have been painted white and studded
with upholstery tacks for a one-of-a-
kind, high-end result.

RENTER
Jen Chu

PROFESSION
Set designer and decorator

LOCATION
Fort Greene, Brooklyn

TYPE
Two-bedroom, 630 square feet

the window as open as possible, and balances all of the storage/office
space along the right wall.

■ STYLE—People don't usually think of highly decorative styles as a
technique for making a space seem bigger, but the dark accent colors, the
high-contrast details, and the ornate bed frame all work to stretch the
boundaries of this small room. Playing with scale like this can be refresh-
ing and, when well executed, can give a modest room a grander, more
luxurious feeling.

Jen calls her bedroom her "tree house" because the window looks right into the upper branches of a maple that houses many squirrels and birds. The long upholstered headboard and the framed artwork balance out the busy shelves that line the opposite wall.

A wall-mounted accordion mirror (just out of the frame) swings into action over the slim makeup station with a clear glass container by the window, and the upholstery tacks lining the windowsill can be clearly seen here. They echo those on the shelf edges.

THE PLATFORM BEDROOM

Tiffany and Alex Hillkurtz's home in an old meat-tenderizing factory feels big, but most of the space is overhead, toward the immensely tall ceilings. When they moved in this was a raw space, and they decided that rather than fit their bedroom into the open living area, they would build up over an existing wall and create a bedroom nearly fifteen feet in the air.

- LAYOUT—A loft bedroom should be installed as far away as possible from the nicest features of the apartment. The couple had originally considered putting theirs nearer the window on the other side of the room, but it would have overshadowed their main sitting space and cut the light from their windows. A loft, while great to be on, is not so great to be under, and dark, quiet spots are the best place to put one.

- STYLE—To make sure that the platform integrated with the rest of the room and didn't become overwhelming, Tiffany and Alex left the warm, natural wood finish and sealed it with polyurethane, for an even more honeyed color. This tied the color of the bedroom in with the exposed brick wall behind it.

KEY INGREDIENTS
- Platform bed
- Modular staircase
- Pipe railing

OWNERS
Tiffany and Alex Hillkurtz

PROFESSIONS
Film editor (Tiffany);
Illustrator (Alex)

LOCATION
North Hollywood, Los
Angeles

TYPE
Studio duplex, 1,200 square
feet

THE OFFICE BEDROOM

Katie Ryan moved into this house with four friends and ended up getting the old office as her bedroom—with its tall, dark brown bookshelves intact. Just out of art school, she was undaunted and set about turning the former work space into a posh little bedroom that expertly tweaked the existing constraints to enhance the sense of size.

- LAYOUT—Katie positioned the bed in the middle of the only wall without a door or a window. She then decked the serious-looking shelves with pictures, artwork, and found objects—not just books—for a relaxed feeling.

- STYLE—While the dark wood cases make the walls look taller, Katie wanted to balance them so they did not overwhelm the room. The answer was to make the floor a colorful focal point, to keep the viewer's eyes moving around the space.

ABOVE LEFT This richly colored lamp is paired with a friend's artwork. While these digs are very modest, and most of the possessions came from garage sales and flea markets, what transforms their bedroom most is the care Katie's taken with the objects and artwork that fill the walls and shelves—many of which were made by friends and classmates from the MFA program at UCLA. As opposed to machine-printed posters and other items that people buy simply to provide decorative cover, the art in this home feels authentic and alive.

ABOVE RIGHT The shelves are filled, not cluttered. Every little space has something interesting in it, and it's all been carefully arranged. Heavier objects balance lighter ones, and denser areas balance open ones.

These bookshelves were built-ins meant for an office, but as a bonus they appear to extend the height of the bedroom walls. The pendant lamp in front of the window adds light at night and visually bridges the two dark bookshelves. Kilim rugs like this add warmth and pattern to a floor. They typically cost less than tufted rugs, come in simple patterns that are traditional but work well in a modern environment, and have rich colors.

RENTER
Katie Ryan

PROFESSION
Artist

LOCATION
Mount Washington, Los Angeles

TYPE
Two-bedroom, 1,400 square feet

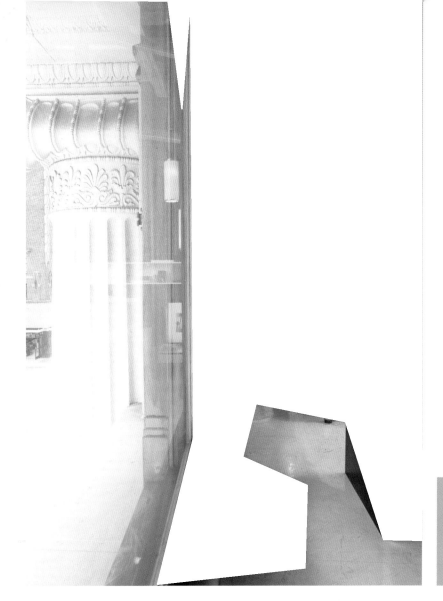

THE ALCOVE BEDROOM

In the past decade, downtown Los Angeles has improved as a place to live, and young people have been taking advantage of low rents in what were once banks and office buildings. While the architecture outside is often impressive, the insides have been wiped clean of any character.

This apartment demonstrates what can be done with a blank slate. Using his photographer's eye, the local IKEA, and great skill with light construction, Alex McClain has built a home for himself that feels spacious and cool.

- LAYOUT—This bedroom used to be a small alcove open to the rest of the studio apartment. To add privacy and storage, Alex fabricated the tall wardrobe, positioning it as a fourth wall to the bedroom, with its back to the living room just beyond. Centering the bed not only makes it easier to climb in or to change the sheets, but it also balances the larger shape

ABOVE The resident plays with scale, balancing his relatively smaller furnishings against the oversize features of the apartment. Here, the huge pillars outside the old bank building make his bedroom seem small and strike a dramatic contrast with the modern interior.

OPPOSITE Horizontal wall-mounted storage acts as both headboard and nightstand in front of the oversize portrait (which the resident painted from a photograph of a friend). The black wall sucks in a ton of light and immediately makes the space smaller and warmer, but the portrait restores a surprising feeling of scale and dispels the sense of emptiness over the bed.

TELEPHONE

RENTER
Alex McClain

PROFESSION
Photographer

LOCATION
Downtown Los Angeles

TYPE
Studio, 690 square feet

of the wall behind and affords a decorative moment on either side with lighting, storage, and artwork.

■ STYLE—While this studio doesn't have a lot of floor space, it does have high ceilings and very harsh industrial textures, so it needed softening and grounding to make the bedroom feel comfortable. The big move was coating one entire wall with black chalkboard paint and then painting a large portrait over the top.

OPPOSITE To illuminate the dark-walled room, pendant lamps are clustered near one wall, and even the "headboard" houses small lights inside it. Bright white and soft gray sheets, as well as the large frame on the bedside photograph, provide even more contrast and balance to the dark wall.

ABOVE Because the space is well finished and highly styled, visitors can't tell that almost everything here was purchased in the IKEA discount section, taken apart, and then put back together in a new way. The wardrobe, for example, is composed of lengths of countertop stood on their ends and wrapped around Pax cabinets. The countertop is reversible, with one white side and one dark side, so the resident faced the white side toward the bed and the dark side toward the living room. The open doors give an idea of just how much storage there is for clothing, as well as for cleaning supplies and even a vacuum.

thoughts on bedroom colors

When I was younger, I wanted my bedroom painted in bright reds and yellows. As I get older, my desire to make my bedroom a calm retreat from the busy world has grown, and my understanding of how color works has grown, too. I now recommend only cool colors to clients who wish to paint their bedrooms, and follow that advice with this explanation.

There are, generally speaking, two types of colors: warm colors and cool colors. Warm colors come from the red and yellow side of the color wheel and are stimulating.

Cool colors, on the other hand, come from the blue and green side of the color wheel, are calming and focusing, and promote activities like reading, working, or sleeping. Thus these colors are particularly good for bedrooms.

Most people want their bedrooms to be cozy and equate this with a warm color, just as I used to. But when they consider the full range of cool colors (grays, blues, purples, greens), they find that some of the most elegant and attractive bedrooms are filled with cool colors.

The bedrooms here all wonderfully demonstrate the cool color range in lighter tones that help reflect light and visually expand the walls of a room. They are tremendously restful and will promote the soundest sleep. And they will also support the sexiest of bedroom encounters.

Deep-blue bedding and curtains work well with the brown bed frame and accents. These darker colors do contract the room, but they also lend drama and make it cozy.

Small doses of color liven up a room and provide a touch of warmth for an overall cool palette. This glass bracelet collection spills out across an entire plate at bedside, and looks good enough to eat.

OPPOSITE This bedroom goes against all
my cool color principles, but it's stunning
to look at. The strong pink here was
meant mainly to take the edge off the
rough brick wall in this former commercial
space, and it works.

ABOVE Whites and grays in subtle grada-
tions have a calming effect.

RIGHT A few black accents stand out
against a white-and-gray backdrop but
not in a busy or overbearing way.

Greens pop just enough against the white to be interesting, but not overstimulating.

Whites and off-whites, mixed together, provide brightness as well as dimension. Pure white, while not technically a color, has a cool quality and can be mixed with color to either remain cool or to turn warm. Here the mix is largely cool.

thoughts on bathrooms

The best companion to a standout small bed-room is a standout small bathroom. My favorite bathrooms are those that are light and open, have a good spatial flow, and are easy to get into and out of, all of which can be challenging in a small space. When I first moved to New York, I lived in an apartment with a raised bathtub in the middle of the kitchen; I had to step up on a chair to climb into it every morning. I vividly remember pulling the thin plastic shower curtain around me as the weak stream of tepid water flowed out of the showerhead and I started my day. That was not a great bathroom!

The bathroom where we live now is much nicer, but it's still nothing to write home about. The ones here are. Each makes great use of the space, has something special to recommend it, and suggests a short list of tips and sources worth passing on (see page 286).

Small bathrooms offer the chance to get a little crazier with the decor. Here, silver wall paint shimmers in just the right (minimal) amount.

RIGHT The two glass walls of this roomy shower maximize light, and the skinny, horizontal tiles make it seem wider than it actually is.

BELOW This bathroom vanity was made from a flea market table that was painted, topped with marble, and retrofitted to accommodate a sink.

ABOVE LEFT With a commercial sink this large, it makes sense to add some storage inside the basin itself. These two baskets adhere directly to the surface of the re-porcelained vintage piece.

LEFT Not having to open a door saves space. Simple, open storage keeps bathroom necessities at hand—and under control.

OPPOSITE This bathroom's green stone tiles and the wood cabinetry and floors were meant to make it feel like a forest; the rest of the fixtures, including the minimal stainless-steel toilet, visually recede.

ABOVE A towel-rack radiator in the same color as the wall is a subtle but super-functional touch that adds no clutter to the room.

RIGHT This simple sink and vanity are attached to the wall and contain an impressive amount of stuff in a compact space.

LEFT AND OPPOSITE In an unusual arrangement, this bathtub lies just beyond a glass wall, which also encloses a shower, thus squeezing two minirooms into one small footprint. And while some bathtubs claim much larger footprints than they need, this one has very thin sides, so it takes up less space without sacrificing a good soak. The layers of nature-inspired color add to the soothing quality of the room.

BELOW Attached to the wall, this vanity assumes a light appearance and offers room underneath for things like a step stool and a wastebasket.

ABOVE Floor-to-ceiling mirrors enlarge this space dramatically, while white medicine cabinets create areas of calm in the center of the wall.

RIGHT This small bathroom is made much larger with ample inset ceiling lighting, mirrors, and an extra-long shower curtain, which has been installed at the ceiling to make the room seem taller. Another space-expanding trick used here? Setting the large marble floor tiles diagonally, which adds dynamism as it breaks up the perpendicular lines and makes the tiles appear wider.

BELOW Metal accents, like this compact, decorative towel hook right beside the tub, are some of the only non-white things in the room. Hardware doesn't have to be large or overly decorative. Though it is often a little harder to find, there are many sources for efficient hardware that will get the job done beautifully.

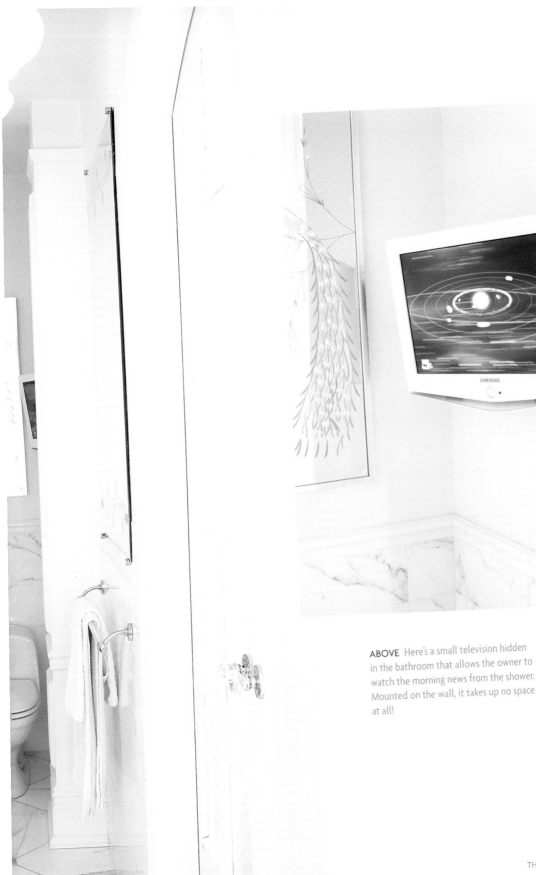

ABOVE Here's a small television hidden in the bathroom that allows the owner to watch the morning news from the shower. Mounted on the wall, it takes up no space at all!

BELOW Many homes have hidden spaces between beams in the walls that can be exploited for small-space storage opportunities.

OPPOSITE AND ABOVE Continuous tile surfaces provide the cleanest appearance for bathrooms—on top of being the easiest to actually clean. In this room, a green tile stripe not only adds an interesting visual element that draws the eye upward, but it also extends out of the room, down a hallway, and into the kitchen, unifying those utilitarian spaces.

smart
home offices

If you work at home, getting your office in shape is priority number one. Even if your primary work space is elsewhere, it is important to have an area of your own that's dedicated to your professional life. This is the goal of a home office: honoring your work and contributing to your success as an individual, whether you are an actor, a writer, a filmmaker, a manager, a financier, or a mom.

In a small residence, having a separate room for a home office is a rarity, of course, and the challenge lies in creating one that provides you with everything you need while you're working, without disrupting your home's flow when you're not. While there's no one right way to achieve this, there are three essential factors for a functional and practical home office:

1. Space (and permission) to spread out and make a mess

2. Easy-access storage for tucking things away

3. Some degree of privacy, even if only the turning-your-back-to-the-room variety

OPPOSITE Once a windowless storage room, this home office got a dramatic lift from a coat of white paint, new windows, and loads of natural light.

ABOVE This office is tucked under a platform bed. Built entirely of plywood units that join storage with structure, it was inspired by the work of Japanese architect Shigeru Ban. This great little grotto resides in a studio apartment that is on full display in the bedroom chapter.

Above all, a home office should inspire you to sit down and open a book, or jump on the computer and check out your favorite blog—by yourself. In this way, it is the least social room in your house.

The following offices range from entire rooms loaded with custom bookshelves to a tiny second-hand desk tucked under a staircase—but each one is used daily, and is an intensely personal solution.

GENERAL TIPS:

■ **GO WIRELESS.** Eliminating electrical cords (or at least hiding them from view) is the single fastest and most dramatic visual improvement you can make in an office space.

■ **DESIGN AROUND THE DESKTOP.** Traditional desk units rarely maximize the uniquely shaped and sized areas in home offices. Start with an unattached desktop, then fill in the space beneath it with rolling file cabinets and bins in the combination that best suits your needs. I've seen people custom-cut doors, kitchen countertops, and plywood to fit their funky small spaces to great effect, and with a custom piece that goes wall to wall, you'll get far more usable surface area and a clean, uncluttered look.

■ **CHOOSE A QUALITY CHAIR.** If you work at home, it probably requires sitting, and often for long stretches of time. The right chair is crucial not only for your comfort but also for supporting healthy posture and contributing to better health. Adequate lumbar support and adjustable seat height are two important criteria.

ABOVE Modestly thrown together, this office has all this dress designer needs: dual screens, proper keyboard height, a comfortable chair, good lighting, and a big enough wall on which to pin plenty of inspiration.

OPPOSITE Sunny and bright, this modern office was the nicest room in the house. The white-painted furniture and floor against the yellow wall make a dramatic statement, and this affordable solution transformed an old, industrial space.

LEFT The deep desktop provides both an expansive work surface and ample, unobtrusive storage. The liberal use of glass and other translucent materials maximizes the room's natural light, bouncing it around in every direction.

■ TIP A glass-topped table does more than reflect light. Just lift the glass, slide a piece of printed fabric or a length of patterned wallpaper underneath, and replace the glass. Voilà, instant makeover.

OPPOSITE Amid the fairly simple furnishings, Kelly has created several "moments," ranging from the practical (books) to the inspirational (totems, photographs). Even in an office, art and whimsy are must-haves.

THE COMMAND STATION OFFICE

When it comes to carving out space for a home office, the ability to see potential in unlikely places is a tremendous asset. This room was originally a windowless pantry, cluttered with old cabinets and a washer and dryer—miles away from the sunny oasis it is now. But designer Kelly Van Patter wanted her office next to the kitchen and dining area so that she could create a "command station"–style office where she could work on projects alone or with others, using the three rooms at once.

■ LAYOUT—To transform the space, Kelly first knocked down a wall that separated this room from the kitchen, then installed three large windows overlooking the pool area. She stashed a vertical washer and dryer in a small closet built into one of the remaining walls, while a second closet holds sliding shelving for all of her appliances and dry goods. Because the

KEY INGREDIENTS

- Wall-to-wall double desktop
- New windows for maximum natural light
- Generous built-in electronics storage

room contains the back entrance to the house, she positioned the bulk of the office along the outer wall so that people don't have to walk through the middle of it to get into the house; this outward orientation all but eliminates the need for electric lighting during the day.

- STYLE—The dark floor, sea-green desk, and bright chairs and rug warm up this airy space and make it inviting. At night, a vintage ceiling fixture, a row of track lighting, and a streamlined task lamp chase out evening shadows and keep the room from seeming to grow smaller.

OWNER
Kelly Van Patter

PROFESSION
Green interior and production designer

LOCATION
Highland Park, Los Angeles

TYPE
Two-bedroom, 1,500 square feet

For such a stylish office, this room has very affordable bones. The desk is made of glass-topped painted plywood and has aluminum legs and trim; its height was calculated to allow store-bought rolling files to slip underneath. The owner added even more storage in the form of simple wall-mounted display boxes above.

THE WALK-IN CLOSET OFFICE

This office is tucked away in a studio apartment. It was originally a walk-in closet, but the owners, Yiming Wang and Xian Zhang, both passionate photographers, decided they wanted a place to house their art supplies more than they needed additional clothing or kitchen storage. The result reveals how to steal space for an office *and* how to spend almost no money making the conversion.

- LAYOUT—As with every room in this book, extra space here was found not by looking for it where it isn't but exploiting it where it *is*—in this case, overhead. Three rows of long, thin shelves mounted on simple brackets make use of the vertical space. To maximize their work area, Yiming and Xian had a solid wood door cut down for a desktop that fits the space perfectly. While many people believe that built-in fixtures are possible only for upscale projects, simple DIY work like this can be just as effective, and certainly cheaper.

ABOVE Photo frames carry the unfinished-wood theme even into the decorative details, which reinforce it as a conscious style choice.

OPPOSITE Nothing softens the edges of a work space—both literally and figuratively—like a rounded, open doorway. Unfinished wooden boxes make excellent modular storage devices—they can be mixed and matched to your heart's content.

OWNERS
Yiming Wang and Xian Zhang

PROFESSIONS
Photographer (Yiming);
Financial analyst (Xian)

LOCATION
Hell's Kitchen, New York City

TYPE
Studio, 500 square feet

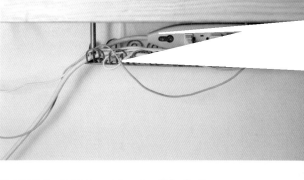

OPPOSITE The final defining element is the two matching chairs that are relatively inexpensive versions of Mart Stam's famous design from the 1920s, which Yiming found in two totally different places (a flea market and curbside!). Their bold, black-and-steel construction is dramatic enough to capture the attention, but light enough that they barely take up any visual space.

■ TIP Furniture with a more skeletal design (less solid and blocklike) is ideal for small spaces.

ABOVE The ingredients here are all simple lumberyard fare, but it's worth noting that the shelves are solid wood and not plywood. In addition to the natural grain being all the "finish" the wood needs, thick pieces like this not only have a heavier, more substantial appearance, but they are also rigid enough to carry more weight and require support on only two sides.

ABOVE RIGHT A simple basket hung beneath the desk does a spectacular job of keeping the wires organized and the desks uncluttered. Since you can see this office from the rest of the apartment, it's important to avoid exposing any awful cord-spaghetti.

■ STYLE—Having spent a good deal of money buying and renovating their apartment, Yiming and Xian had to pare down somewhere. They went for a simple palette and a natural, purely functional style. All the wood is unfinished, as are the multiple IKEA storage boxes, which gives the room a warm, honey glow. The walls were kept white to match the rest of the apartment, and a nearly frameless floor-length mirror has been installed to make the room appear bigger and to ward off any sense of claustrophobia.

THE MINI LIBRARY OFFICE

Perched on the top floor of a small house, this standout office gathers light from two big windows along the side and surrounds visitors with long shelves of books, yet everything is perfectly organized. The owners, Leslie Maslow and Alan Dorsey, patiently redid everything in their home from the ground up, enlisting an architect to help. For Leslie, a writer, the most important room was this office. She wanted to have "a jewel box of a room" where she could easily disappear all day long.

■ LAYOUT—Seclusion is the organizing principle here. With the desk facing the wall and surrounded by beautiful built-in bamboo cabinetry on every side, potential distractions are all but eliminated. The two windows on the right let in natural light from the side, which prevents glare (or shadows) on the work surfaces. Open upper shelves allow the owner to see her entire book collection (neatly organized), and the lower shelves are paneled, hiding away drawers, files, and other unsightly objects.

ABOVE LEFT Using white Corian countertop as a desk surface is unusual and inspired. Though expensive, Corian is warm to the touch, bright white, and has a very thin, light line, distinguishing it from most other countertops. It doesn't stain, and you can easily sand out any scratches or dings. It can be cut to fit in any way, making it ideal for filling custom spaces.

OPPOSITE The strong lines of these horizontal wraparound bamboo shelves make this compact office seem wider than it actually is, while keeping masses of books organized. Beautiful, affordable, and an easily renewed resource, solid bamboo has become a popular "green" alternative for the home. Separated by heavy sliding doors from the rest of the house, the office easily becomes a soundproof retreat.

OWNERS
Leslie Maslow and Alan
Dorsey

PROFESSIONS
Writer (Leslie);
Cabinetmaker and wood
artist (Alan)

LOCATION
Cobble Hill, Brooklyn

TYPE
Three-bedroom, 1,800
square feet

■ STYLE—In order to pack a lot into this office while maintaining a light, open feeling, the architect employed a few simple, easily adaptable tricks. The biggest one, of course, is that placing a white Corian desktop against white walls brings them together seamlessly and amplifies the light from the two windows. Next, the upper shelves stop short of the ceiling by about six inches and the lower cabinets sit above an inset at the floor. These spaces give the cabinets the appearance of floating on the wall and allow for visual flow over and under the large masses. Third, the architect included a line of rope lighting under the upper lip of every shelf and cabinet, which illuminates the shelf below and ensures that the room is bathed in light at all times.

THE CURTAIN OFFICE

Walking into this apartment is like visiting a movie set: The bright Los Angeles sun streaming through creates layers of light. It is quiet and peaceful, and blissfully simple.

Like the rest of the studio, the office is heavily influenced by the Asian background of the owner, Manson Fung, as well as by the time he spent working in Japan, and every detail has been refined down to its essence.

- LAYOUT—With only one window to provide light for the whole apartment, Manson eschewed dividing walls in favor of sheer curtains, and he positioned them so that his daytime activities (studying and working) would take place nearest the window; his bed is tucked in the farthest space for privacy and darkness, and the living room occupies the middle ground. Manson keeps his storage needs at a minimum, which allows for much more open space; what he does have is contained behind the glass doors of the cabinet by his desk.

OPPOSITE Although this apartment faces north and has only one window, the available natural light is amplified by the white walls and pale furniture, and sheer curtains allow light to pass through the entire apartment. The curtains are the owner's own ingenious creation. For the rods, he spray-painted narrow-gauge copper plumber's pipe white and attached it to the ceiling with copper mug hooks (which are easy to screw in by hand). Then he sewed the curtains to fit his space exactly, adding a pole pocket along the top of each to hide the pipes from view.

ABOVE LEFT In such a spare space, any little thing can look like clutter; stacking objects makes them instantly neater and more pleasing to the eye.

RIGHT This type of design sensibility depends as much upon empty space as filled space: The negative space between the objects allows the eye to flow comfortably from one to the other.

OPPOSITE With a few simple curtains, Manson made three rooms out of one. The view from the living room to the office shows just how much light can pass through curtains, while they still offer a strong visual separation.

RENTER
Manson Fung

PROFESSION
Designer

LOCATION
Hollywood, Los Angeles

TYPE
Studio, 600 square feet

■ STYLE—The style here is very architectural—simple to describe but much harder to execute. In addition to keeping possessions and furniture to a minimum, the owner has chosen only pieces that have slender frames. An all-white palette like this can be severe, but what warms up this room is the inclusion of light-brown hues in the wood furniture, the cardboard table, and the owner's lush potted plants. Against such a clean backdrop, little colorful touches, like the Post-it notes on the wall, really draw the eye.

This office acts like a palate cleanser. Not everyone can live this minimally, but it is inspiring when done well. In particular, the way Manson has created space with light and extremely modest materials is a great object lesson.

THE IKEA HACKER OFFICE

Alex McClain has done a remarkable number of beautiful things with IKEA elements. He takes the concept of hacks, as these transformations of IKEA items are called, to a whole new level. The entire apartment is sharply finished and pulled together.

■ LAYOUT—The studio, a small loft space in an old bank building, was a blank slate, so positioning the wide white desk against the black wall was a strong way of signaling a different zone and giving a huge, open feeling to that side of the room. As opposed to positioning the desk perpendicularly, this treats the desk as a visual element that connects the windows to the other side of the room.

■ STYLE—Black walls are rare in small spaces, because black paint absorbs light and tends to make spaces feel smaller—even more so when it is chalkboard paint, which has a soft matte finish that acts like a magnet for the light. Why does it work so well in this space? This apartment's open floor plan has a lot to do with it. Since there's no privacy or true boundary for the office, the huge black wall actually helps to define the nook, dramatically setting off the photo mosaic and giving the side of the room a more contracted, cozy feeling, which helps Alex focus his thoughts on the work in front of him.

OPPOSITE The owner has flawlessly fit together all the affordable elements with some skillful DIY work. The desk is a countertop set on metal legs, and the cabinets on either side are kitchen cupboards and wardrobe drawers. The owner's other showstopper—the artwork made from a photograph he took of a friend—also looks like a million bucks, but it cost him only a few using a Web program.

■ TIP Use PosteRazor.com to enlarge and tile any image, making it printable on individual sheets; then tack each one up to make your own oversize collage.

ABOVE LEFT A tiny bonsai tree injects a dose of color and life into the graphic, hard-edged work space.

ABOVE RIGHT The owner's laptop, which also acts as the hard drive for his desktop monitor and keyboard, remains tucked underneath the desk in two metal brackets when he's not taking it on the road: a fantastic space-saving and clutter-reducing trick.

OWNER
Alex McClain

PROFESSION
Photographer

LOCATION
Downtown Los Angeles

TYPE
Studio, 690 square feet

THE CORNER OFFICE

The owner of this home, Kelly Giesen, possesses a wealth of information, and every solution is based on either a special source or a space-saving tip that she discovered during four renovations. In addition to taking up very little space, this office has the added benefit of hiding the owner's work and disappearing at night, so that the bedroom is all that's seen.

■ LAYOUT—Kelly doesn't believe in having a lot of furniture and prefers getting built-ins whenever possible in order to maximize square footage. This corner office can house a desk, a chair, four shelves, and her audio system in a truly minuscule space. Because she went to great pains to blend the molding and paint colors with the rest of the room, you'd never know that it is a completely new addition.

OWNER
Kelly Giesen

PROFESSION
Interior designer

LOCATION
Upper West Side, New York City

TYPE
One-bedroom, 725 square feet

Another trick to this office's success is its corner placement. Corners contain a lot of unused space, but they are very important visually—as natural points for our eyes to pause as they move around the room. Building in a feature that has the appearance of a continuous wall results in the best of both worlds: usable space and no visual clutter.

- STYLE—The ceiling gets a bright white (Benjamin Moore's Decorator's White), the walls get a softer white (Benjamin Moore's Glacier White), and the trim, which comprises this office, gets a cream white (Benjamin Moore's Ballet White); this unifies the vintage pieces with the new ones and softens the overall appearance. Using multiple whites in this way also adds tremendous sophistication: The different shades allow the eye to play back and forth between them and cast a far warmer glow.

Backed by mirrors, these office doors reflect nothing but light. While the office is new construction, the doors are Parisian antiques with etched-glass insets that the owner found at ABC Carpet & Home. The wallpaper surrounding the office is also highly reflective—it's made of tiny glass beads.

FUTAKI FABRIC FADDIE '05

HOMAGE TO A TYPEFACE

THE SLIDING OFFICE

This home office is nestled behind a door within a bedroom, and it shows how sweet and simple a work space can be. All the necessary elements—computer, bookcase, task light, even artwork—have been boiled down to their essentials.

- LAYOUT—This type of office is highly dependent on wireless technology. The keyboard and laptop connect with a Bluetooth signal, which allows them to live on the desk with no strings attached; the laptop can then easily be picked up and moved to any room in the house.

- STYLE—The all-white color approach helps enlarge the room, but it also provides a very effective backdrop for the non-white accent pieces: the professional drummer's stool in place of an office chair and the vertical bookcase, which is almost sculptural (and a very clever storage solution).

ABOVE Without wires tying everything together, this hardly feels like a work space.

OPPOSITE This is a great design for a desk: It expands when in use, collapses when not, and offers much better surface heights for keyboarding (low) and reading (high).

OPPOSITE A tall, narrow bookcase marks off the back "wall" of the office and eliminates the need for wall-mounted shelves, which can eat up more visual space.

ABOVE An office spot behind a bedroom door can be a good idea, because it's quiet during the day and tucked away from the rest of the home, but it should be minimal and somewhat camouflaged: When home offices get too busy, it's best to set them up farther away from the sleep area.

LEFT This wireless Apple setup not only looks fantastic, it is about as minimal as it can be. This is also a good pitch for going laptop instead of desktop. With all the power that slim laptops now have, one really doesn't need anything more than this in most homes.

a few more
quick offices

While working on this book, I found a bunch of remarkable tiny offices that were fashioned out of necessity in odd places. Not all of them require much explanation, but they were all uniquely personal and inspiring to look at. I didn't want you to miss them.

This outbuilding lies at the end of a yard behind a Santa Monica bungalow. The resident, a fashion designer, needed an office out of which to run her clothing company and decided to set up shop here rather than rent someplace farther away.

OPPOSITE Tucked in a closet on the side of the resident's living room, with a bright yellow door frame and vintage fabric hung from the ceiling inside, this lovable office hides all her books, papers, and materials from view.

ABOVE Unlike most offices, this one is in a dining room, with the desk facing out. This makes perfect sense, however, because the desk is so attractive and the setup allows for nicer flow around the furniture. While some offices are serious and secluded, this one is a good example of a more relaxed, homey style.

RIGHT This collection of eyeglasses is surprising but lovely in how it conveys the passion of the owner, a screenwriter, and all the time spent working in this office.

TIP When there's no room for a full office, look for a desk with a drop leaf, or a hutch that you can close when you're finished working.

BELOW This storage system holding all the little books and containers was actually found in a bathroom, but it's perfect for a tight office as well. The owner mounted thin metal IKEA shelving and wall rails to hold a ton of supplies neatly and visibly up the wall.

ABOVE Corkboard covered in brown FLOR tile brings strong contrast and almost instant usability to this wall above a desk space tucked into a kitchen. Dressing up corkboard is always a good idea. It rarely looks good enough by itself inside a home.

LEFT This tiny studio apartment has no room for an office, but the resident was able to fit under the staircase this little desk, where he can pay bills and work on his computer. Since the theme of his home is nautical (he calls his home the SS *Waverly*), a small secretary similar to a captain's desk was the perfect choice.

thoughts on desk organization

Like kitchens, home offices are working spaces, and they are at their best when they show that off. They should be well stocked, well lit, and easy to clean up. To achieve this, there are two basic requirements: good cord control and easily visible inspirational materials and supplies.

CORD CONTROL—This is an ongoing challenge, but the secret here is to get your cords below eye level and under your desk. Whatever it takes, just get them out of there as fast as you can!

- First, get your cords to the back and down, away from your desktop. This may mean cutting a hole in your desktop or snaking your cords down the rear.

- Second, get all cords *up* under the desktop, either by strapping them in with Velcro or catching them in a basket or a wire channel, which will allow them to run close to the desk.

- Make it easy to get to your cords in order to move or change them. Don't let them run behind anything you can't move.

- Use zip ties to bind your cords together so that they can be moved as one mass; these are easily found at computer stores and places like the Container Store, or a really good online source is CableOrganizer.com.

(continued on page 221)

Plain, wall-mounted shelves serve as both storage and inspiration boards in this tiny bedroom office.

This little desk is tucked between the owner's kitchen and front door. What makes it so successful is the angled surface and the built-in shelves that provide attractive overhead storage.

(continued from page 218)

STORAGE INSPIRATION—The designers Charles and Ray Eames famously had multiple walls in their office on which they constantly rearranged photographs and other elements when working on a project. There should always be a space at your desk that's set aside for inspiration. (With a really tight space, this area may be overhead.)

■ Have some type of bulletin board where you can pin up notes, drawings, or other ephemera to ignite your thought processes.

■ Use open shelving for inspiration and easy reference.

For me, out of sight really is out of mind. While it can be nice to have cabinet doors and a way to file some things out of sight, I like to be able to view the things I work with most often. There are many companies that sell nice boxes, binders, and bins for open storage. Two of my favorites are Bigso of Sweden and Russell and Hazel of Minnesota.

The owner of this office cut a narrow channel near the back of his desk to allow for several concealed points of entry for the various cords. From the front, the cords on this desk are completely invisible.

RIGHT If you curate your belongings carefully, storage becomes style. These three shelves are made of painted wood, with contrasting decorative nail heads hammered along the edges. The repetition of these hundreds of small shapes creates a strong visual frame for all the belongings and helps them to feel contained instead of too busy.

OPPOSITE This amazing bulletin board above a desk is adorned with all the elements for a wedding dress the owner had made for her wedding.

petite
children's
rooms

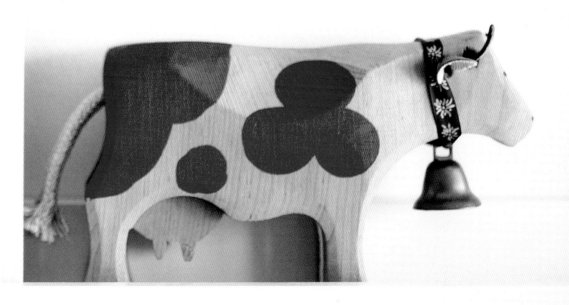

One of the first things people will ask when you announce that you're expecting a child is, "When are you going to move?" No matter how big your place, more room, it is assumed, is required for children. When Ursula was born, Sara Kate and I were living in a 250-square-foot studio, and people told us we were crazy not to move.

But not everyone has a choice. We didn't, and you know what? We were fine. In fact, I would credit that first year with making us better parents, because there was absolutely no escape, and we got to know our baby really well. That experience changed my thinking about kids' rooms forever.

Particularly with children, small is cool. Children are very adaptable and infinitely imaginative, and they require their parents more than space. They are noisy, however, which means the one thing you'll need—eventually—is a separate room with good soundproofing. But it doesn't need to be big: It just needs to be comfy and filled with love.

The rooms in this chapter all fit the bill. They are comfortable and lovingly decorated spaces where children can rest and play and be close to their parents, because there's usually not enough room for much separation.

We eventually did relocate to a slightly bigger apartment when Ursula was one and a half and beginning to move around a lot. By that time, we could afford it and were eager for a change, but some of our habits never left us. We've always kept the toys to a minimum and cycled out old ones whenever a good new one came in; we've been diligent about passing on her old clothes to friends and returning those that we've borrowed for her; and we've made it a priority to teach her to clean up after herself. Our home feels a lot bigger for it.

OPPOSITE While some children clamor for bunk beds—any bunk beds—these built-in bed cubbies go above and beyond: They are one part summer camp, one part *2001: A Space Odyssey*, and 100 percent smart small-space solutions.

ABOVE A strong wall color can personalize a child's room while offering a vibrant backdrop for art and toys.

GENERAL TIPS:

- ■ MINIMIZE YOUR PURCHASES. I've already said this, but it bears repeating—because even if you are careful and don't buy a lot for your child, friends and family will give gifts and you'll end up buried under a pile of useless toys and objects. Keeping the amount of child-related stuff to a minimum will make your life easier and your child's life a lot calmer. You'll also have more room.

■ INVEST IN STORAGE THAT'S EASY TO USE. Good storage is a must with children, because even before they grow old enough to start putting things away, you'll need to do so, often with your eyes closed and your hands full. Dressers that are easy to open and bins or baskets with open tops are useful.

■ LET YOUR IMAGINATION RUN WILD. A room for a child should be youthful, childlike, and fun. Since they're not designing the rooms themselves (yet), it's up to you to find and express your own inner child. Take advantage of this creative opportunity and amaze yourself. This room might just become your favorite in the house.

■ DESIGN TO MUFFLE LIGHT AND SOUND. Darkness is important for children when falling asleep, and quiet, while also helpful, is even more important for parents who don't want to hear a baby's crying at full volume. Blackout shades will solve the former, and plenty of textiles (rugs, blankets, upholstery, artwork) will help with the latter, if your walls aren't thick enough to do the job on their own.

ABOVE LEFT Children's rooms are for having fun in! This ceramic lamp of two birds resting would be an odd choice for a grown-up's room, but it's perfect for this two-year-old girl.

ABOVE RIGHT In addition to the bird lamp, the owner of this room hung these whimsical silk flowers from the wall. Every detail is a feast for a child's eyes.

OPPOSITE A quiet reading spot in the corner of Ursula Gillingham-Ryan's small nursery is created by a small-scale vintage "nursing chair." While the window illuminates during the day, round party lights create a soft glow at night.

THE CAPSULE BUNK BED

For kids, a closed-in sleeping environment can feel comfortable rather than confining. By squeezing two twin beds and loads of storage into a ten-by-ten-foot space, the owners, Andrea Robbins and Max Becher, created a cozy getaway for their boys. Although the capsules look little from the outside, the two single mattress beds inside feel roomy.

- LAYOUT—The footprint of this room is small, and two beds side by side would have been a difficult fit, especially with the boys' bedside tables and all their belongings. The extra space in this room is vertical, so a bunk bed made a lot of sense. This one cleverly integrates into the room's architecture. Each child also benefits from a semiprivate space of his own—a great compromise in a small home. The cubbies have shelves, their own lights, and even small windows out onto the exterior hallway.

- STYLE—This room's modern—even futuristic—design is softened both by the curves of the cubby windows and by the sky-blue walls inside them. Simply changing the color palette as the children grow will render the room much more adult and sophisticated over time.

ABOVE LEFT No storage opportunity is wasted: Even the rail above the ladder supports a small shelf for boxes and toys.

ABOVE A mirrored door in the middle of this picture hides the entrance to the bunk beds; everything is designed to blend into the walls.

RIGHT Wall niches provide unobtrusive storage—and decoration—in the individual cubbies.

BELOW Through small windows in the hallway, the parents can check on each child without actually entering the room, or the children can peek out.

ABOVE Inside, a narrow ladder offers access to the upper bunk.

OWNERS
Andrea Robbins and Max Becher

PROFESSIONS
Artists and professors

LOCATION
Soho, New York City

TYPE
One-bedroom, 1,000 square feet

OWNERS
Stephanie Doucette and
Mark Robohm

PROFESSIONS
Dress designer (Stephanie);
Drummer (Mark)

LOCATION
Chelsea, New York City

TYPE
Two studios, combined, 780
square feet

KEY INGREDIENTS

- Tall doorways, window, and ceiling
- Two entrances
- High window louvers for light and air

THE BREAKTHROUGH NURSERY

As a child grows and more room is needed, it's highly unusual to find it right next door! Stephanie Doucette and Mark Robohm were living in a very small studio apartment (380 square feet) when their son was born. After a year of living happily together, they decided they needed a separate room for the baby and started looking around. When they learned that their neighbor was moving out and was willing to sell her apartment, the couple bought it and went to work joining the two small spaces into one nice, medium-size apartment.

■ LAYOUT—The shape of this room was chosen for purely functional reasons. It had to be long and narrow so that it would fit between the master bedroom and the adjoining apartment beyond. Because the ceilings and windows are nice and high, the owners highlighted this extra

LEFT This room is completely new, due to the renovation, but Mark and Stephanie have filled it with antiques, like the vintage Pastoe shelves; handmade items, like the rocker; and family hand-me-downs so that it has character and spirit. While most pieces in this nursery are light in color, the cowhide rug provides a dark focal point.

OPPOSITE In a stroke of small-space genius, the couple repurposed a crib side that wasn't being used; now it makes a charming statement as a decorative clothing rack. The brick doorway behind it also stands in as a frame for baby Wilson's first artwork.

LEFT Looking into the nursery, the outline of the doorway that joins the owners' two small apartments can be seen on the brick wall. One thing that makes this nursery work is that the owners haven't relied on "nursery" furniture to decorate it. Of particular note, the rocking chair by Jason Lewis is a beautiful, practical piece of furniture that is rare to see in a nursery. The owner has reupholstered it in luscious fabric. Their son will be able to take it to college one day; this chair will last a lifetime.

OPPOSITE The changing table and crib by Netto Collection were found on eBay for a fraction of the going price. The couple was initially drawn to the design elements—the white lacquer finish and wenge accents—but each piece also offers a lot of storage.

space by designing very tall doorways and adding high louvered windows to the far wall, which increase the circulation in the nursery and pull light into the hallway beyond.

■ STYLE—The pleasing style of this room combines Mark's crafty, country roots and Stephanie's fashion-business orientation. The walls are soft white and blue to create a sense of airiness, while the furnishings, which are grown up, bold, and stylish, add pops of color and contrast to the walls.

THE ARCHITECTS' UNDER-NURSERY

While parents usually tower over their children, it is rare that they also sleep right over their heads. But for Sara and Juan Matiz, a parents'-loft-on-top, kids'-room-on-bottom design was the best way to make use of their narrow floor space and unusually tall ceilings. The snug, small bedroom and nursery for their two children (yes, two children!) keeps the little ones right under their noses, but the sliding panel door keeps the space dark and quiet, even when the parents are up with guests.

- LAYOUT—Inspired by the clean lines of Renzo Piano and Santiago Calatrava, the couple created areas of density and areas of openness throughout the apartment, with all the surfaces light and bright, and spots of color and a dark floor for balance. The children's room itself accommodates only a crib and a toddler bed, but that's plenty, because all the storage is smartly contained along the left wall, on shelves and behind doors. A clothes closet sits under the stairs inside the room.

ABOVE Architects seem to know all the tricks when it comes to beautiful construction at the lowest price. For their cabinetry, the owners used a mix of custom and IKEA pieces: A close look reveals that the cabinets (IKEA) are wrapped in thick wood frames (custom), while the doors (IKEA) have been upgraded with designer pulls—playful ones in the kids' room and minimal ones in the outer room. A combination of open and closed storage lets the family decide which items go on display and which get hidden.

ABOVE A sliding door gives the children a quiet and private place to sleep at night—even though their room is smack in the middle of the apartment—and allows the parents to quickly hide away any messes when guests drop by. The owners chose to make this room as tiny as it is to allow for the dining and living areas to be much bigger, so that the kids also have all the space they need during active hours.

■ STYLE—A nice mix results when parents design their kids' rooms to be fun and childlike but keep their common spaces adult and sophisticated. Creating distinctions between areas is important; it not only allows for more dramatic stylistic shifts, but it also helps to contain children's belongings, which can easily overrun the home.

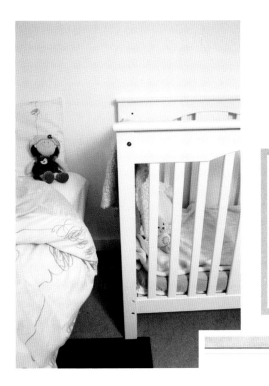

OWNERS
Sara and Juan Matiz

PROFESSION
Architects

LOCATION
Chelsea, New York City

TYPE
Loft, 450 square feet

OPPOSITE Inside the children's room, the soft FLOR tiles, green shelving, and good lighting create a world unto itself.

ABOVE The baby's crib and the toddler's bed are both in the room, and very near each other, but despite the cramped quarters, the children love it. They're also really good with each other from growing up in such close proximity.

RIGHT The stairs to the right are designed to take up less space than traditional stairs by climbing more quickly (hence, the two-step steps), but, being made of metal, they don't require as much extra support and provide a large closet with even more storage inside the children's room.

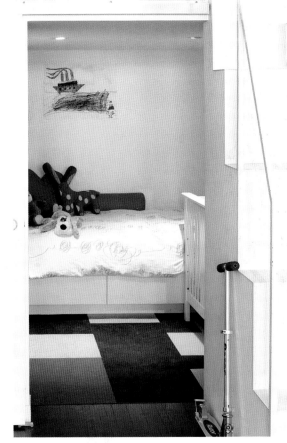

THE PRINCESS BEDROOM

Jennifer Ward recently finished giving her daughter Parker's room a make-over. (Parker was going through a major princess phase and wanted a more grown-up space.) Her mother took advantage of the opportunity to clean out the room and move a lot of belongings to storage; then the walls were painted a luminous, not-too-deep purple that makes the space feel vibrant and fun.

- ■ LAYOUT—Unusually, there is another entrance to the apartment behind Parker's bed. To work around this unused and slightly unsettling feature, her mother installed a gauzy canopy whose thicker back layer conceals the door completely. Turned sideways and tucked inside the canopy, the bed fills the space perfectly and acts like a built-in, making both the sleeping nook and the overall room feel larger. With a long room like this, it makes sense to arrange the bed perpendicular to the room's longest wall, because the two contrasting features will balance each other.

- ■ STYLE—This room was inspired by the books of Oliver Jeffers: In fact, the deep purple wall paint was a direct match from a color in one of Jeffers's books. This is a great example of how a kid's room can become "bigger" and grow with the child.

ABOVE LEFT Behind-the-door storage is great for kids' rooms, because when it's not so neat, the open door will hide it from view. Hooks should be positioned at a height a child can easily reach.

ABOVE In a child's room, scale is everything. Here, the billowy canopy around the bed makes the sleeping area seem larger and adds a lot of drama to a fairly simple layout. Although it seems like a daring choice at first, purple actually made a lot of sense here. While warm colors tend to be overstimulating for bedrooms, and cool colors too grown up, purple, a combination of blue (cool) and red (warm), gives the room a rich and fanciful feeling that's just right for a growing child.

OPPOSITE With a vivid color like this one, you don't need a lot of wall art to make the room feel lively—and white and black accents really pop against the purple.

ABOVE White accents like the mirror, the letter wall hanging, and the rug are also powerful counterpoints to the darker walls.

RENTER
Jennifer Ward

PROFESSION
Imagination agent and creative director

LOCATION
Carroll Gardens, Brooklyn

TYPE
Two-bedroom, 1,150 square feet

ABOVE This canopy was made from ten white IKEA curtain panels attached to two curtain rods near the (also white) ceiling—a no-commitment project you can easily remove when it's lost its charm. The residents also installed a chandelier inside the canopy, so that the bed area would glow with light.

LEFT Almost any old thing looks great with a white-paint makeover. This mirror was once a faux-wood-grain reject left on a curb, but now it's a highlight of the room.

OPPOSITE Simple wire storage crates coated with black chalkboard spray paint echo the dark metal bars of the bed, store a lot without taking up much room, and almost disappear when filled with books and playthings.

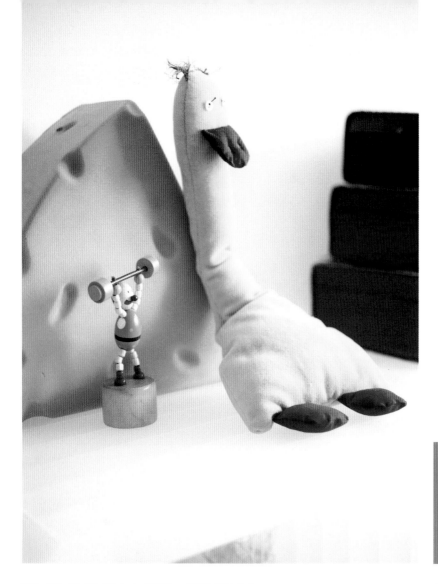

THE ROOM-TO-GROW CHILDREN'S ROOM

By keeping the walls clear and the storage near the floor, it's possible to open up a room like a big sky. This is three-year-old Ella Joy's bedroom, designed by her mother, Tina Roth Eisenberg, a web designer and blogger. Due to her no-nonsense Swiss heritage and her love of clean design, Tina wanted this room to be neat, easily organized, and clutter free.

■ LAYOUT—Children's rooms differ from all others because they need a dedicated open space in the middle for play. This room has a nice big rug in its center, and all of Ella's toys, books, and dolls are stored next to it on shelves and in bins, so that they are easy to pull out and put away again.

■ STYLE—The tasteful incorporation of primary-colored objects creates a look that's pleasingly clean and calm but still child-friendly and fun. Three of the walls are painted a bright white, and an accent color of soft blue

OPPOSITE Knowing that children's rooms should change along with them, the owner has employed a host of easy-to-alter solutions: A picture rail lets her swap out artwork without making new nail holes, and modular Cubitec shelving provides a neutral and rearrangeable backdrop for the most-used items.

ABOVE Teaching kids to organize their toys by color can be a fun learning activity. Bonus result: The room will look neater!

■ TIP Provide clear storage and a place for everything. At such a formative stage in their lives, children, with their parents' help, will gain confidence and establish lifelong habits as they learn that maintaining the "home" is easily done.

OWNERS
Tina Roth Eisenberg and
Gary Eisenberg

PROFESSIONS
Graphic designer and blogger
(Tina); Kitchen designer (Gary)

LOCATION
Downtown Brooklyn, New
York

TYPE
Two-bedroom, 1,185 square
feet

covers the walls behind the bed, embracing it and suggesting the feeling of being in a nook. Clear white shelving, white bins, and white frames soften anything that isn't important and reduce visual clutter. In contrast, the big red numbers pop, the stuffed animals come to life, and the eye travels around the room from highlight to highlight. There's actually a lot happening here, but the way in which the objects are organized and placed against such a clean, light background makes the room seem simpler than it is.

OPPOSITE With young children, it's important to always be thinking one step (or one year) ahead. This convertible IKEA bunk bed can sleep two children and also can be flipped to become a single bed with a canopy for an older child later on.

ABOVE A broad, striped rug outlines Ella's play area (and cushions her knees).

■ TIP Look for easy-to-clean rugs in natural fibers and flat weaves.

This little desk-and-chair set slips in by the window to give Ella a grown-up place to work. Because the chair fits precisely into the table's curves to form a cube, this piece could easily serve as a side table or a nightstand once Ella's grown too large to sit in it.

THE LULU ROOM OF BIRDS

This was a totally fun project that involved clearing out a walk-in closet and transforming it into a bedroom fit for our two-year-old daughter, Ursula. The person responsible for the magic was my mother-in-law, Karen Gillingham, a stylist in Los Angeles, who fell in love with the idea of collecting birds and vintage objects to create a sophisticated little girl's room where Ursula could stay when we visited her.

■ LAYOUT—Starting with the bed, which had been in the family for many years, and was able to fit sideways at the back of the room, Karen retrofitted a bookshelf to carry all the books and clothes Ursula would need for short stays. Karen then added plenty of light to brighten the windowless room while removing the doors in favor of floor-to-ceiling curtains that give the room additional light and even more of a storybook feeling. Storage here is generous but finite. Ursula is expected to be neat!

ABOVE Simple shapes delight the eye. This vintage toy and ceramic bird tray filled with hearts and butterflies contrast large and small.

OPPOSITE Seen through the billowing curtains, the repurposed closet is barely recognizable, and the cozy room draws one in. Curtains in small spaces are a fabulous replacement for doors. They add style, allow more light, and take up no solid space. Doors would have made this room claustrophobic.

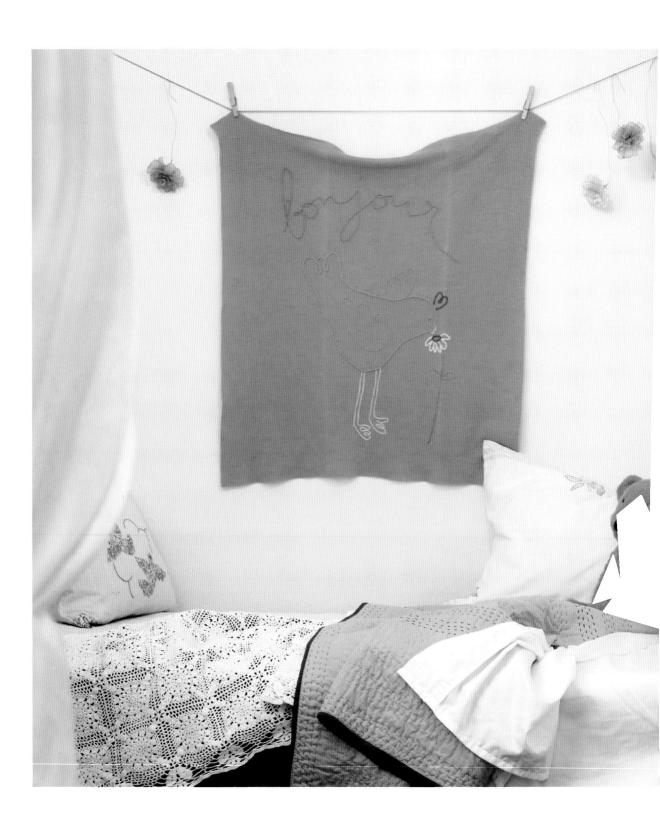

OPPOSITE Layers of color provide contrast and visual complexity. When a strong theme is used to unify all the elements, there's no reason for everything to be too matchy-matchy.

ABOVE The other important element of this room is that everything has a strong handmade feeling. These hand-sewn pillows and bedspread show enough of how they were made to allow a small child to imagine doing it him- or herself.

OWNER
Karen Gillingham

PROFESSION
Food stylist

LOCATION
Studio City, California

TYPE
Two-bedroom bungalow, 2,000 square feet

ABOVE Ursula was so proud of her room she wanted to pose for the camera with her friend Giraffey.

RIGHT The wool crewelwork whorls of this Menagerie rug tell their own story of a jungle bustling with animals.

OPPOSITE The detail of this lamp from Urban Outfitters is truly impressive. While the birds look in every direction (to speak to the others), the vintage metal table has been softened and brightened by a linen handkerchief. A fresh magnolia blossom completes the picture.

■ STYLE—Everywhere one looks in this room, small birds are to be found: underfoot, on the wall, on shelves, and in the whimsical lamp that was the coolest thing Ursula had ever seen. The ongoing collection of bird shapes and images comes from many sources. The inspiration, however, was the round rug, found at Anthropologie, which also set the warm color palette of yellows with accents of red and green.

thoughts on storage

I hate the word "storage." It seems so lifeless, as though it refers to places you put things you don't want, don't use, and don't really want to see again. This approach seems particularly problematic when it comes to children, who live in the present, love to be active, and would rather use something than put it away. This means that storage shouldn't be too deep or too hidden. It should be easy to access and full of useful, desired objects instead of rejected things crammed away.

For this reason, consider open containers and shelves and old-fashioned solutions like hooks, bins, and wide-mouth bottles—the simpler the better. Here are a few more storage ideas that may help you think about it in a new way and might even inspire a new name for it.

These built-in shelves were designed to go around a desk in a home office, but it turns out they leave just the right amount of open space for a sleek crib (whose slats echo the shelves). No one wants to be hunting around for things while holding a baby, so open storage like this is ideal for an infant's room.

OPPOSITE Replacing cabinet doors with curtains (or adding them to open shelving) makes access easier for little hands with developing motor skills.

▥ TIP A few cute patterned curtains mounted with tension rods can turn an old bookcase into a second closet for toys and games.

ABOVE Open bins are light and durable and easy to access (which increases the likelihood that a child will pick up after him- or herself). They're also perfect for repurposing to hold clothing or art supplies for older children.

RIGHT Companies that primarily supply schools often include smart (and durable) storage solutions with their toys and games. This wood block set from Community Playthings is sold with a matching wheeled wooden cart that makes it easy for children to put things away.

BELOW Hooks are great storage devices—particularly old ones. They make the most of otherwise unused areas and the slimmest of spaces. The key is simply to hang some at the right height for your little ones.

ABOVE This old computer found a useful second life as a music system in the nursery. The screen allows the family to easily select songs, even in the dark.

OPPOSITE Built-in shelves are the best way to create storage that fits seamlessly into a room. These brightly painted shelving units visually melt into the wall, providing clean frames for an assortment of art, shoes, books, and animals.

thoughts on nursery lighting

Lighting is always important, but in a child's room it can be especially challenging, because you need many different kinds of illumination for sleeping, reading, and changing diapers at 3 a.m. Additionally, these rooms are often the smallest, so there's not always enough space for a floor or table lamp. A better alternative: a handful of different wall- or ceiling-mounted light sources, all hooked up to dimmers that are easy to reach and covered in playful shades that can be made easily. Here are a few creative suggestions that are perfect for little rooms.

Beyond the gaggle of paper lanterns, the DIY cord that powers them runs down the corner, while a modern ceramic lamp sits next to the changing pad. Each light source is on a dimmer and provides a very different light for a variety of occasions.

BELOW In this nursery, large paper lanterns hang from the ceiling, with a single light in the center hooked up to a dimmer, creating instant ambient lighting with a dreamy, cloudlike quality.

OPPOSITE For a smaller-scale example of lantern lights, string bulbs with mini paper lanterns to help mark off doorways or sitting areas. Their soft, luminous glow is good for reading by—and for falling asleep by.

ABOVE Here, a wall-mounted outdoor light is the perfect solution for bunk bed cubbies with no floor or table space for a freestanding lamp.

resources

INTRODUCTION

ALEX MCCLAIN, PAGE 9

- **WALL SHELF AND LIGHTS:** IKEA
- **CURTAIN:** Made by McClain's sister from fabric from Jo-Ann Fabrics, joann.com

VANÉ AND CHAD BROUSSARD, PAGE 10

- **THROW BLANKET:** DesignHouse Stockholm, designhousestockholm.com
- **WHITE LACQUER CABINETS WITH WALNUT ACCENT:** built by Solid Solutions, Brooklyn, NY; shop primed and painted with Benjamin Moore, satin Impervo white, benjaminmoore.com; pulls, Sugatsune SN95, sugatsune.com
- **ORANGE CHAIR:** IKEA
- **SOFA:** Petrie from Crate&Barrel, crateandbarrel.com
- **COFFEE TABLE:** Mash Studios Lax series, mashstudios.com
- **RUG:** FLOR tile, flor.com
- **PILLOWS:** Jonathan Adler, jonathanadler.com and Hable Construction, HableConstruction.com.
- **SIDE TABLE:** Design Within Reach, DWR.com
- **SMALL BIKE BASKET:** Design House Stockholm, designhousestockholm.com
- **TASK LAMP:** Artemide Tolomeo, artemide.us
- **ARTWORK:** porcelain, Jonathan Adler, jonathanadler.com; babyhead body and feet, Kirsten Steglich; vase with yarn ICFF, designboom, designboom.com; Mushroom and wood pieces Etsy, Etsy.com
- **CLEAR PLEXI FRAMES:** Crate&Barrel, crateandbarrel.com

OPPOSITE, CLOCKWISE FROM TOP LEFT A home filled with items crafted by the hands of artists is an inviting home, indeed. These views all come from one house, where the owners took time to source each element. The wood on the stairs is solid cherry, runs throughout the house, and was chosen by the architect, Delson or Sherman. The unique pendant chandelier was designed by Omer Arbel for Bocci. The glass window was designed by a local craftsman, Frank Close. The wooden bird is a classic from the 1950s, designed by Kristian Vedel.

LAURA AND TIMOTHY DAHL, PAGE 11

- **STUFFED DOG:** Etsy, etsy.com
- **MIRROR:** Craigslist, NYC, craigslist.com

BETHANY OBRECHT, PAGES 12–13

- **LAMPSHADES:** Target, target.com
- **SIDEBOARD:** early 1960s Motorola record player
- **PAINT:** Martha Stewart for Lowe's, lowes.com
- **CHAIRS:** David's Consignment, Baltimore, MD, reupholstered in Duralee Fabrics, duralee.com

KELLY VAN PATTER, PAGE 15

- **TASK LAMP:** yard sale
- **TOTEMS:** Native American
- **SWIRLY VASES:** from Nemadji, Minnesota
- **TV RACK:** Best Buy, bestbuy.com
- **SMALL FLAT FILE:** Bisley, bisleyusa.com

YIMING WANG AND XIAN ZHANG, PAGE 16

- **RACKS:** Grundtal, from IKEA
- **BLACK MARBLE TILE:** The Home Depot, homedepot.com

TIFFANY AND ALEX HILLKURTZ, PAGE 17

- **LUMBER AND ALL SUPPLIES:** The Home Depot, homedepot.com
- **STAIRCASE:** Arke Karina Modular Stairway Kit, arkestairs.com

QUICK ENTRANCES

DAVID ALHADEFF, PAGES 18–20

- **LIGHT UP NUMBER ONE:** Area 51, area51seattle.com

- **VASE WITH DRIED FLOWER:** Golden Calf, 319 Wythe Avenue, Brooklyn, NY 11211, 718.302.8800

- **LUGGAGE:** JUNK, Williamsburg, 197 North Ninth Street, Brooklyn, NY 11211, 718.388.6981

VANÉ AND CHAD BROUSSARD, PAGE 21

- **CABINETS:** IKEA wall cabinets hung low with custom top and Sugatsune pulls

- **TEXTILE:** Anthropologie, anthropologie.com

- **TOTE:** threepatatofour by little bird, threepotatofourshop.com

- **ARTWORK:** Camilla Engman, camillaengman.com; Jen Corace, jencorace.com; Amy Helfand, amyhelfand. com; Letterpress cards from Port2Port Press, port2portpress.com; John Murphy, white framed print, johnmurphyart.com

THE LONG HOUSE ENTRANCE
VANÉ AND CHAD BROUSSARD, PAGES 24–25

- **COATRACK:** designHouse Stockholm, designhousestockholm.com

- **CANDLESTICKHOLDERS:** Roost, roostco.com

- **CABINETS:** IKEA wall cabinets hung low with custom top and Sugatsune pulls

- **TEXTILE:** Anthropologie, anthropologie.com

- **TOTE:** threepatatofour by little bird, threepotatofourshop.com

- **RUG:** Bolon on the floor, bolon.com

- **ARTWORK:** Camilla Engman, camillaengman.com; Jen Corace, jencorace.com; Amy Helfand, amyhelfand. com; Letterpress cards from Port2Port Press, port2portpress.com; John Murphy, white framed print, johnmurphyart.com

THE HALL OF MIRRORS
MICHELLE AND TRACY MCCORMICK, PAGES 26–29

- **COWHIDE RUG:** street vendor

- **MIRRORED CABINET:** a gift from the last designer Tracy worked with, Stamps and Stamps, stampsandstamps. com

- **LITTLE MIRRORS:** Modern 50, modern50.com and flea markets: Rose Bowl, Pasadena, Santa Monica

- **DISCO BALLS:** Brimfield Antiques Show, brimfield.com

- **COWBOY PICTURE:** Antiques Row, Philadelphia, PA

- **PEACE FINGER HANDS:** flea markets, ebay.com, Garygibson.com, and from Tracy's dad, Frank

- **CHANDELIER:** auction from the old Ambassador Hotel in Los Angeles

THE OUTSIDE ENTRANCE
SARA KATE AND MAXWELL GILLINGHAM-RYAN, PAGES 30–31

- **VINTAGE HOOKS:** Olde Goode Things, oldegoodthings.com

- **SHOE RACK:** The Container Store, containerstore.com

- **METAL BASKET:** bike basket

- **LARGE COIR MAT:** Ace Hardware, acehardware.com

- **ARTWORK:** Emily Payne, Emilypayne.net

THE HANDMADE HALLWAY
STEPHANIE DOUCETTE AND MARK ROBOHM, PAGES 32–35

- **ARCHITECT:** Josh Fenollosa helped design the space, brownfenollosa.com

- **WOOD HOOKS, WOOD FOR LADDER, AND WALNUT LOFT:** Live Wire Farm, livewirefarm.com

- **DESK CHAIR:** found on street, Herman Miller, hermanmiller.com

- **CREDENZA:** found on street

FIVE MORE FAST ENTRANCE IDEAS

DAVID ALHADEFF, PAGE 37

- **LIGHT UP NUMBER ONE:** Area 51, area51seattle.com
- **VASE WITH DRIED FLOWER:** Golden Calf, 319 Wythe Ave, Brooklyn, NY 11211, 718.302.8800
- **LUGGAGE:** JUNK, Williamsburg, 197 N 9th Street, Brooklyn, NY 11211, 718.388.6981

NOAH POSNICK, PAGE 39, ABOVE RIGHT

- **KEY RACK:** oak slab from CharlesandMarie.com

COZY KITCHENS AND DINING ROOMS

LESLIE MASLOW AND ALAN DORSEY, PAGES 40–41

- **ARCHITECT:** Delson or Sherman Architects, delsonsherman.com
- **CHAIRS:** Jens Risom side chairs, dwr.com

VANESSA WARD AND BRIAN KREX, PAGE 42

- **STOVE:** Viking 36" with hood, vikingrange.com
- **VENT:** custom, professional vent
- **DISHWASHER:** Miele 24", miele.com
- **SINK:** 30" Franke professional sink, 12" deep, frankeksd.com
- **FAUCETS:** Dornbracht Tara Classic, dornbracht.com
- **WATERFILTER:** Franke, frankeksd.com
- **UTENSIL BAR:** Hafele, hafele.com
- **MARBLE:** backsplash, Calcutta gold 1¼" cut down to ¾", self-picked at New England Stone, newenglandstone.com
- **CABINETRY:** custom shop-sprayed enamel by Polygon Projects, 204 Van Dyke Street Suite 3, Brooklyn, NY 11231-1038, 718.852.4466

- **PULLS:** Sugatsune, sugatsune.com
- **ZEBRAWOOD:** zebrawood veneer
- **FLOOR TILE:** Concordia from Stonesource, stonesource.com
- **DESIGN:** Bangia Agostinho, Anshu Bangia, William Agostinho, bangiaagostinho.com

MICHELLE AND TRACY MCCORMICK, PAGE 45

- **TABLE AND CHAIRS:** IKEA
- **ART:** flea markets
- **CANDLESTICKS:** Soap Plant, soapplant.com

BLACK-AND-WHITE PREWAR UPDATE

YIMING WANG AND XIAN ZHANG, PAGES 46–49

- **CABINETS, STOVE TOP, FAUCET, AND RACKS:** IKEA
- **SINK:** Expo
- **DISHWASHER:** Bosch, boschappliances.com
- **BLACK MARBLE TILE:** The Home Depot, homedepot.com
- **CARRERA MARBLE:** from shop in Brooklyn, NY
- **DINING TABLE:** Urban Outfitters (antique), urbanoutfitters.com
- **CAKE STAND:** Anthropologie, anthropologie.com

THE FAMILY-FRIENDLY KITCHEN
VANESSA WARD AND BRIAN KREX, PAGES 50–53

- **FRIDGE:** SubZero 36"
- **STOVE:** Viking 36" with hood, vikingrange.com
- **VENT:** custom, professional vent
- **DISHWASHER:** Miele 24", miele.com
- **SINK:** 30" Franke professional sink, 12" deep, frankeksd.com
- **FAUCETS:** Dornbracht Tara Classic, dornbracht.com
- **WATERFILTER:** Franke, frankeksd.com
- **UTENSIL BAR:** Hafele, hafele.com
- **MARBLE:** backsplash, Calcutta gold 1¼" cut down to ¾", self-picked at New England Stone, newenglandstone.com
- **CABINETRY:** custom shop-sprayed enamel by Polygon Projects, 204 Van Dyke Street Suite 3, Brooklyn, NY 11231-1038, 718.852.4466
- **PULLS:** Sugatsune, sugatsune.com
- **ZEBRAWOOD:** zebrawood veneer
- **FLOOR TILE:** Concordia from Stonesource, stonesource.com
- **DESIGN:** Bangia Agostinho, Anshu Bangia, William Agostinho, bangiaagostinho.com

THE SET DESIGNER'S ECO KITCHEN
KELLY VAN PATTER, PAGES 54–55

- **CABINETS:** birch ply cabinets with eurohinges and pulls by Amarok
- **COUNTER:** remnant ¾" Venini marble, honed
- **BACKSPLASH:** white subway tile (seconds) from B&W Tile, bwtile.com
- **SINK AND FAUCET:** KWC, kwcamerica.com
- **GLASS JARS:** IKEA
- **ISLAND:** IKEA butcher block with custom stainless top wrapping the wood top; custom stainless shelf on top of lower wood shelf
- **CARPET:** FLOR, flor.com

- **STOOLS:** Naota Fukasawa Aluminum stools from MoMA Store, momastore.org
- **CEILING FIXTURES:** Smith and Hawken (out of business)
- **GARBAGE CAN:** SimpleHuman, simplehuman.com
- **DISHWASHER:** Bosch, boschappliances.com
- **STOVE:** Maytag, maytag.com
- **PAINTS:** cabinets, Glidden, Eastern Lighthouse, glidden.com; walls, Benjamin Moore, Mother of Pearl, benjaminmoore.com

THE SUNNY, RECYCLED KITCHEN
JUSTINA BLAKENEY, PAGES 56–59

- **ALL ITEMS:** flea markets, Craigslist, garage sales, Blakeney's grandmother, and The Home Depot, homedepot.com

THE VERSAILLES KITCHEN
KELLY GIESEN, PAGES 60–63

- **MARBLE:** Calcutta gold, ABC Stone Trading, Queens, abcworldwidestone.com
- **CEILING PENDANT:** Olde Goode Things, oldegoodthings.com
- **CUSTOM CABINETS:** with antique glass
- **FRIDGE:** 30" refrigerator drawer, Marvel, lifeluxurymarvel.com
- **FREEZER:** 24" refrigerator/freezer. Marvel, lifeluxurymarvel.com
- **DISHWASHER:** 18" Miele dishwasher, miele.com
- **STOVE:** 30" Viking stove, vikingrange.com

OPPOSITE, CLOCKWISE FROM TOP LEFT: Yiming Wang, Luis Caicedo, Bethany Obrecht, Kelly Van Patter, Michelle and Tracy McCormick, Maxwell Gillingham-Ryan, Manson Fung, Bethany Obrecht and Maxwell Gillingham-Ryan, Justina Blakeney.

THE UNDER-BED KITCHEN
MAT SANDERS, PAGES 64–67

- **PLATES WITH STRIPES:** Bed Bath & Beyond, bedbathandbeyond.com

- **SUGAR AND FLOUR TINS:** flea market

- **PAINT:** blue on wall, Benjamin Moore Old Navy, benjaminmoore.com; gray, Ralph Lauren Tudric Pewter, RalphLaurenHome.com; seafoam, Ralph Lauren Sea, RalphLaurenHome.com

- **FLEA MARKETS:** The Garages (Greg), 15th Street and Sixth Avenue, NYC; Brooklyn Flea, Brooklyn, NY

- **BEDDING:** Jonathan Adler for Bed Bath & Beyond, bedbathandbeyond.com

THE JEWEL-BOX KITCHEN
GENNADI MARYASH AND TERENCE SCHROEDER, PAGES 68–71

- **CABINETS:** custom made, shop spray-painted wood with Hafele pulls, hafele.com

- **COUNTER AND BACKSPLASH:** white Corian, dupont.com

- **FAUCET:** Hans Grohe, hansgrohe.com

- **MIRROR WALL:** custom

- **SHELVES:** Rakks, rakks.com

- **WHITE BINS:** IKEA

- **DOOR:** covered in mohair with upholstery system underneath (plastic channels)

- **DISHWASHER:** Fisher and Paykel, fisherpaykel.com

- **COOKTOP:** Verona, veronaappliances.com

- **REFRIGERATOR:** Summit, summitappliance.com

- **APPLIANCE SOURCE:** Krups Kitchen & Bath, krupskitchenandbath.net

- **FAN:** Modern Fan Company, modernfan.com

- **TABLE:** antiques store

- **CHAIRS:** eBay, ebay.com

- **FABRIC:** Baranzelli, baranzelli.com; Pindler and Pindler, pindler.com, Scalamandre, scalamandre.com

- **CARRERA TILE:** Nemo, nemotile.com

- **FIXTURES AND FITTINGS:** Flaminia, ceramicaflaminia.it

THOUGHTS ON SMALL DINING ROOMS
NOAH POSNICK, PAGE 73

- **DINING TABLE:** West Elm, westelm.com

- **CHAIRS:** Bellini from Conran, conran.com

- **PAINT:** Chocolate brown, Benjamin Moore, benjaminmoore.com

- **PENDANT LAMP:** CB2, cb2.com

- **ART:** Avedon images cut out of "Woman in the Mirror"

- **FRAMES:** Adorama, adorama.com

MICHELLE AND TRACY McCORMICK, PAGE 74, PAGE 75 (ABOVE)

- **TABLE AND CHAIRS:** IKEA

- **ART:** flea markets

- **CANDLESTICKS:** Soap Plant, soapplant.com

- **ZEBRA RUG:** Rose Bowl flea market

DAVID ALHADEFF, PAGE 75, RIGHT

- **GLASS VASES:** The Future Perfect, thefutureperfect.com

- **CHAIRS:** Louis Ghost Chair by Philippe Starck for Kartell, Kartell.it

BETHANY OBRECHT, PAGES 76–77

- **TABLE:** Horseman Antiques, 351 Atlantic Avenue, Brooklyn, NY 11217, 718.596.1048

- **CHAIRS:** David's Consignment, Baltimore, MD; reupholstered and repainted—fabric by Duralee Fabrics, duralee.com

- **RUG:** Ballard Designs, ballarddesigns.com

- **LAMPSHADES:** Target, target.com

- **VASE:** CB2, cb2.com

- **SIDEBOARD:** early 1960s Motorola record player

- **PAINT:** Martha Stewart for Lowe's, lowes.com

- **FLOOR LAMP:** Pottery Barn, potterybarn.com

- **CURTAINS:** IKEA

LAURA AND TIMOTHY DAHL, PAGES 78–79

- **CHAIR:** Louis Ghost Chair by Philippe Starck for Kartell, Kartell.it

THOUGHTS ON CABINET DECOR
LESLIE MASLOW AND ALAN DORSEY, PAGES 81–83

- **ARCHITECT:** Delson or Sherman, delsonsherman.com
- **STOVE:** Wolf, wolfstoves.com
- **REFRIGERATOR:** Jenn-Air, jennair.com
- **CABINETS:** custom with wenge wood
- **COUNTER:** Pietro de Cardoza marble

SARA AND JUAN MATIZ, PAGE 84, ABOVE LEFT

- **CABINETS:** IKEA bodies with custom countertop and handles
- **BACKSPLASH:** Walker and Zanger porcelain tile, walkerzanger.com
- **COUNTER:** stainless steel married to a stainless steel sink, North Welding, northwelding.com
- **HARDWARE:** Simon's, simonshardware.com
- **STOVE:** Viking 24", vikingrange.com
- **DISHWASHER:** Bosch, bosch-home.com
- **MICROWAVE:** Dacor, dacor.com

STEPHANIE DOUCETTE AND MARK ROBOHM, PAGE 84, ABOVE

- **CABINETS:** custom-made by cabinetmaker, Budget Cabinets, covered with orange laminate above and with walnut veneer below
- **COUNTERTOP:** one-piece stainless steel countertop, restaurant grade, with drop-in sink from the Bowery in NYC
- **STOVE:** Avanti, flat top electric, avantiproducts.com

STACI BILLIS AND MICHAEL LEBOWITZ, PAGE 84 (LEFT)

- **ARCHITECT:** In Situ Design, Mason Wickham (design) and Ed Wickham (project management), insitudesign.com
- **CABINETS:** custom-built, shop-sprayed wood with Benjamin Moore paints, benjaminmoore.com
- **GAS COOKTOP:** Dacor, dacor.com
- **DISHWASHER:** GE profile, geappliances.com
- **ELECTRIC STOVE:** Jenn-Air, jennair.com
- **COUNTERTOP:** stainless steel thin layer on top of plywood with a wood trim
- **CABINET HARDWARE:** Sugatsune edgepull, sugatsune.com

STEPHANIE DOUCETTE AND MARK ROBOHM, PAGE 86, CENTER

- **CABINETS:** custom-made by cabinetmaker, Budget Cabinets, covered with orange laminate above and with walnut veneer below
- **COUNTERTOP:** one-piece stainless steel countertop, restaurant grade, with drop-in sink from the Bowery in NYC
- **STOVE:** Avanti, flat top electric, avantiproducts.com

STACI BILLIS AND MICHAEL LEBOWITZ, PAGE 87, ABOVE

- **ARCHITECT:** In Situ Design, Mason Wickham (design) and Ed Wickham (project management), insitudesign.com
- **CABINETS:** custom-built, shop-sprayed wood with Benjamin Moore paints, benjaminmoore.com
- **GAS COOKTOP:** Dacor, dacor.com
- **DISHWASHER:** GE profile, geappliances.com
- **ELECTRIC STOVE:** Jenn-Air, jennair.com
- **COUNTERTOP:** stainless steel thin layer on top of plywood with a wood trim
- **CABINET:** hardware Sugatsune edgepull, sugatsune.com
- **FRIDGE:** KitchenAid, kitchenaid.com

SARA AND JUAN MATIZ, PAGE 87, BELOW

- **CABINETS:** IKEA bodies with custom countertop and handles
- **BACKSPLASH:** Walker and Zanger porcelain tile, walkerzanger.com
- **COUNTER:** stainless steel married to a stainless steel sink, North Welding, northwelding.com
- **HARDWARE:** Simon's, simonshardware.com
- **STOVE:** Viking 24", vikingrange.com
- **FAUCET:** Blanco, blancoamerica.com
- **SINK:** Blanco, blancoamerica.com

THOUGHTS ON OPEN STORAGE
DAVID ALHADEFF, PAGES 89, 90, AND 91 (LOWER RIGHT)

- **KITCHEN RACKS:** Grundtal, from IKEA
- **TABLE:** stainless steel restaurant supply on the Bowery, NYC
- **COFFEEPOT:** Bodum vacuum style, bodum.com
- **TEA CUP:** (with blue inside) Redstr Collective Tea Cup, redstrcollective.com
- **STOOL WITH PLEXI TOPS:** The Future Perfect, thefutureperfect.com

TIFFANY AND ALEX HILLKURTZ, PAGE 91, ABOVE AND ABOVE RIGHT

- **METAL BARS:** Grundtal, from IKEA
- **METAL SHELVES:** IKEA

ANTHONY AND HILARY PADGETT, PAGE 92

- **METAL BARS:** Grundtal, from IKEA
- **SHELVING:** Metro Shelving, metro.com

SHARON BORDAS AND DAMON HILL, PAGE 93 ABOVE

- **BUTCHER BLOCK:** IKEA

SARA KATE AND MAXWELL GILLINGHAM-RYAN, PAGE 93 ABOVE AND TOP

- **MIRROR:** Room and Board, roomandboard.com
- **WINE RACK:** Vintage View Racks, vintageview.com
- **CHAIRS:** vintage
- **POT RACK:** Overstock, overstock.com

COMPACT LIVING ROOMS
SARA KATE AND MAXWELL GILLINGHAM-RYAN, PAGE 95

- **PAINT:** Benjamin Moore Eco Spec (walls, China White; trim, Dove White), benjaminmoore.com
- **CURTAINS AND RODS:** Pottery Barn, potterybarn.com
- **RUG:** The Rug Company, therugcompany.com
- **SOFA:** Caravane from Calypso Home, calypso-celle.com
- **ROCKING CHAIR:** SleepyTime by Nursery Works, nurseryworks.net
- **PILLOWS:** Judy Ross, judyrosstextiles.com
- **BOLSTERS:** Purl fabric, purlsoho.com, made by Mathew Haly, thefurniturejoint.com
- **SIDE TABLES:** IKEA
- **SMALL LAMP:** BTC Lighting, btclighting.com
- **WHITE BASKETS:** IKEA
- **SHEEP SKINS:** IKEA (white) and 3 Corner Field Farm (brown), dairysheepfarm.com
- **ARTWORK:** squiggles by Maxwell; landscape by Mary Bayes Ryan; big light ink drawing by Emily Payne, emilypayne.net

VANÉ AND CHAD BROUSSARD, PAGE 96

- **THROW BLANKET:** DesignHouse Stockholm, designhousestockholm.com
- **WHITE LACQUER CABINETS WITH WALNUT ACCENT:** Built by Solid Solutions, Brooklyn, NY; shop-primed and painted with Benjamin Moore, satin Impervo white, benjaminmoore.com
- **PULLS:** Sugatsune SN95, sugatsune.com
- **SOFA:** Petrie from Crate&Barrel, crateandbarrel.com
- **COFFEE TABLE:** Mash Studios Lax series, mashstudios.com
- **RUG:** FLOR tile, flor.com
- **PILLOWS:** Jonathan Adler, jonathanadler.com; Hable Construction, HableConstruction.com

BETHANY OBRECHT, PAGE 97

- **CHANDELIER:** eBay, Australia

JUSTINA BLAKENEY, PAGE 98–99

- **ALL ITEMS:** flea markets, Craigslist, garage sales, Blakeney's grandmother, and The Home Depot, homedepot.com

THE DAYBED LIVING ROOM
SARA KATE AND MAXWELL GILLINGHAM-RYAN
PAGES 100–103

- **PAINT:** Benjamin Moore Eco Spec (walls, China White; trim, Dove White), benjaminmoore.com
- **CURTAINS AND RODS:** Pottery Barn, potterybarn.com
- **RUG:** The Rug Company, therugcompany.com
- **SOFA:** Caravane from Calypso Home, calypso-celle.com
- **ROCKING CHAIR:** SleepyTime by Nursery Works, nurseryworks.net
- **PILLOWS:** Judy Ross, judyrosstextiles.com
- **IKAT PILLOWS:** Andriana Shamaris, andrianashamaris.com

- **BOLSTERS:** Purl fabric, purlsoho.com, made by Mathew Haly, the furniturejoint.com
- **LAWYER'S BOOKCASES:** vintage
- **SMALL LAMP:** BTC Lighting, btclighting.com
- **GLASS TABLE LAMP:** CB2, cb2.com
- **STEREO:** Apple HiFi, apple.com
- **WHITE BASKETS, SIDE TABLES, AND LANTERN:** IKEA
- **SHEEPSKINS:** IKEA (white) and 3 Corner Field Farm (brown), 3 Corner Field Farm, County Route 64, Shushan, New York 12873, 518.854.9695, dairysheepfarm.com
- **ARTWORK:** squiggles, Maxwell; landscape, Mary Bayes Ryan; big light ink drawing by Emily Payne, emilypayne.net

THE COLLECTOR'S LIVING ROOM
MICHELLE AND TRACY MCCORMICK, PAGES 104–107

- **CHAIR:** Urban Outfitters, home section, urbanoutfitters.com
- **BOOKS:** Book Soup, booksoup.com
- **BOOKS:** Hennesy and Ingalls, 214 Wilshire Boulevard, Santa Monica, CA 90401, 310.458.9074
- **SOFA FABRIC:** Larsen, larsenfabrics.com
- **SOFA:** flea market
- **PAINT:** Sydney Harbour Paints, sydneyharbourpaints.com

THE SATELLITE LIVING ROOM
LAURA AND TIMOTHY DAHL, PAGES 108–111

- **SOFA:** Room and Board, roomandboard.com
- **BLACK CHAIR AND OTTOMAN:** vintage
- **SIDE CHAIR:** Room and Board, roomandboard.com
- **RUG:** Monti Rugs, montirugs.com
- **ELEPHANT:** gift from Mom
- **STUFFED DOG:** Etsy, etsy.com
- **MIRROR:** Craigslist, NYC, craigslist.com
- **TABLE MIRROR:** Z Gallerie, zgallerie.com

THE EVERYTHING-WALL LIVING ROOM
VANÉ AND CHAD BROUSSARD, PAGES 112–115

- **THROW BLANKET:** DesignHouse Stockholm, designhousestockholm.com

- **WHITE LACQUER CABINETS WITH WALNUT ACCENT:** built by Solid Solutions, Brooklyn, NY; shop-primed and painted with Benjamin Moore, satin Impervo white, benjaminmoore.com; pulls, Sugatsune SN95, sugatsune.com

- **ORANGE CHAIR:** IKEA

- **SOFA:** Petrie from Crate&Barrel, crateandbarrel.com

- **COFFEE TABLE:** Mash Studios Lax series, mashstudios.com

- **RUG:** FLOR tile, flor.com

- **PILLOWS:** Jonathan Adler, jonathanadler.com and Hable Construction, HableConstruction.com

- **SIDE TABLE:** Design Within Reach, DWR.com

- **SMALL BIKE BASKET:** Design House Stockholm, designhousestockholm.com

- **TASK LAMP:** Tolomeo by Artemide, artemide.us

- **ARTWORK:** porcelain, Jonathan Adler, jonathanadler.com; babyhead body and feet Kirsten Steglich; vase with yarn by ICFF designboom, designboom.comeng; mushroom and wood pieces Etsy, Etsy.com

- **CLEAR PLEXI FRAMES:** Crate&Barrel, crateandbarrel.com

THE INDUSTRIAL LIVING ROOM
DAVID ALHADEFF, PAGES 116–119

- **PILLOWS STACKED ON FLOOR:** ABC Home, abchome.com; Domestic Element, domesticelement.com; and a gift from the launch of *Suede* magazine

- **PIG FIGURE ON FLOOR:** Salvation Army in Seattle, WA

- **PILLOWS ON SOFA:** The Future Perfect, thefutureperfect.com; AG Merch, aandgmerch.com

- **BLANKET ON SOFA:** Indian Blanket, A&G Merch. aandgmerch.com

- **RUG:** Timorous Beasties custom carpet, timorousbeasties.com

- **COFFEE TABLE:** Vintage Table, Carl Chaffee, carlchaffee.com

- **RUBBER STOPPER CHAIR:** Redstr Collective, redstrcollective.com

THE MULTILAYERED LIVING ROOM
LUIS CAICEDO, PAGES 120–123

- **PENDANT LAMP:** Nelson ceiling lamp, Modernica, modernica.com

- **SOFA:** Vicente Wolf, vicentewolf.com

- **PILLOWS:** Bed Bath & Beyond, bedbathandbeyond.com

- **DRAPES:** custom made by Luis Caicedo

- **GRAY FORMICA CONSOLE:** custom made

- **ANTIQUE CHINESE HORSES:** flea market on 25th Street, NYC

- **RUG AND LUCITE TABLE:** Housing Works, housing works.org

- **MIES VAN DER ROHE ORIGINAL CHAISE:** thrift store

- **PILLOWS:** made of recycled oriental rug/velvet, custom made by Luis Caicedo

- **WHITE ACRYLIC SCULPTURE:** flea market on 25th Street, NYC

- **FIRE SCREEN:** found on street

- **TERRACOTTA HEAD:** from Caicedo's former house in Chicago

- **BLACK AQUARIUM STONES IN FIREPLACE:** Petco, petco.com

- **NINETEENTH-CENTURY SILVER BRITISH EMPIRE CHAIR:** Jew Town, Cochin, India

- **COW SKIN VINTAGE VETERINARY CASE:** flea market, Bogota, Colombia

- **ARTWORK:** homeless person sale, 23rd Street, NYC

- **GOLD LEAF CONSOLE:** Housing Works, housingworks.org

- **RESIN CIRCULAR ARTWORK:** Luis Caicedo

- **FRAME:** Housing Works, housingworks.org

- **DECO CHINESE WALL SCONCE:** from a theater, A-1 Antiques, a-1antiquesofnaperville.com

- **OVAL ARTWORK:** Nancy Friedemann, nancyfriedemann.com

- **GOLD PORCELAIN "PAPER BOWL":** Vintage Saks Fifth Avenue, saks.com
- **GOLD MIRROR:** Maxwell Street flea market, Chicago

THOUGHTS ON BOOKSHELVES
VANÉ AND CHAD BROUSSARD, PAGE 125

- **WHITE LACQUER CABINETS WITH WALNUT ACCENT:** built by Solid Solutions, Brooklyn, NY; shop-primed and painted with Benjamin Moore, satin Impervo white, benjaminmoore.com; pulls, Sugatsune SN95, sugatsune.com
- **TASK LAMP:** Artemide Tolomeo, artemide.us
- **PORCELAIN:** Jonathan Adler, jonathanadler.com

VANESSA WARD AND BRIAN KREX, PAGE 126

- **BOOKCASE AND CUSTOM CABINETS:** Rakks, rakks.com
- **PULLS:** Sugatsune, sugatsune.com
- **CLOCK:** wedding present
- **CHANDELIER:** vintage
- **FLOORING:** FLOR tiles, flor.com
- **CHAIR:** Eames LCW

GENNADI MARYASH AND TERENCE SCHROEDER, PAGE 128

- **SHELVES:** Rakks, rakks.com
- **WHITE BINS:** IKEA
- **DOOR:** covered in mohair with upholstery system underneath (plastic channels)

VANESSA AND BRIAN KREX, PAGE 129

- **BOOKCASE:** Rakks, rakks.com

THOUGHTS ON TELEVISIONS AND STEREOS
SARA KATE AND MAXWELL GILLINGHAM-RYAN, PAGE 135, LEFT

- **STEREO:** Apple HiFi, apple.com
- **KNITTING BASKETS:** IKEA

MINIATURE BEDROOMS
TINA ROTH EISENBERG, PAGES 136–137

- **BED:** Min bed from Design Within Reach, dwr.com
- **RUG:** Chiasso, chiasso.com
- **SIDE TABLE:** made from reclaimed beams, custom designed by Tina and Rick Lewis of RG Furniture Design, rgfurnituredesign.com
- **LAMP:** IKEA
- **PILLOWS:** West Elm, westelm.com; House Industries, houseind.com

HILARY PADGET AND ANTHONY HARRINGTON, PAGE 138

- **BED FRAME:** Baltic Birch Ply, furniture grade with hand-applied gel finish
- **TRACK AND CURTAINS:** IKEA (with added weights)
- **BEDDING:** Area, areahome.com
- **MATTRESS:** Sonno, Design Within Reach, dwr.com
- **TASK LAMPS:** IKEA
- **SHELL CHAIRS:** Eames, vintage
- **OFFICE CHAIR:** Eames Management Chair from Room and Board, roomandboard.com
- **SOFA:** Case Study Sofa from Modernica via Craigslist, modernica.com
- **BLUE BINDERS:** Bindertek.com
- **LITTLE STOOLS:** Gilbert from IKEA
- **DRESSERS:** found on street in Okemus, Michigan
- **READING LIGHT:** Lighting by Gregory, lightingbygregory.com
- **TELEVISION:** Sony monitor with Surround Sound speaker
- **BIG PAINTING AND PORTRAIT:** Hilary Padget
- **FAN:** Westinghouse industrial fan

KELLY VAN PATTER, PAGE 139, LEFT

- **SIDE TABLES:** Danish vintage
- **LAMP:** cube lamp by Lampa, lampa.com

JENNIFER WARD, PAGE 140

- **RUG:** Flokati
- **CURTAINS:** IKEA
- **BOOKCASE:** bookcase with legs turned on side
- **CAMERAS:** gathered from road trips across the country
- **BEDDING:** Bed Bath & Beyond, bedbathandbeyond.com

LESLIE MASLOW AND ALAN DORSEY, PAGE 141

- **STONE:** Himarchal stone from India, Nemo, nemotile.com

THE ELEVATED CUBE BEDROOM
HILARY PADGET AND ANTHONY HARRINGTON,
PAGE 142–145

- **BED FRAME:** Baltic Birch Ply, furniture grade with hand applied gel finish
- **TRACK AND CURTAINS:** IKEA (with added weights)
- **BEDDING:** Area, areahome.com
- **MATTRESS:** Sonno, Design Within Reach, dwr.com
- **OFFICE CHAIR:** Eames Management Chair from Room and Board, roomandboard.com
- **SOFA:** Case Study Sofa from Modernica via Craigslist, modernica.com
- **BLUE BINDERS:** Bindertek.com
- **LITTLE STOOLS:** Gilbert from IKEA
- **DRESSERS:** found on street in Okemus, Michigan
- **READING LIGHT:** Lighting by Gregory, lightingbygregory.com
- **TELEVISION:** Sony monitor with Surround Sound speaker
- **BIG PAINTING AND PORTRAIT:** Hilary Padget
- **FAN:** Westinghouse industrial fan

THE DIVIDER BOOKSHELF BEDROOM
NOAH POSNICK, PAGES 146–149

- **TASK LAMP:** Tizio Artemide, artemide.us
- **DESK:** walnut veneer parson's table custom made in NYC
- **CHAIR:** Aeron by Herman Miller, hermanmiller.com
- **FILE:** Sam Flax, samflaxny.com
- **WASTEPAPER BASKET AND BED FRAME:** IKEA
- **CORKBOARD:** Staples, staples.com
- **PAINTING:** Noah Posnick
- **FLOOR LAMP:** Tolomeo by Artemide, artemide.us
- **SOFA:** BB Italia copy in Brandy Valor by McCreary Modern, Inc., ABC Home, abchome.com
- **BOOKCASES:** Cubitec, Design Within Reach, dwr.com
- **CURTAINS AND RODS:** West Elm, westelm.com
- **SHADES SOLAR:** Smith and Noble, smithandnoble.com
- **MATTRESS:** Bloomingdale's, Bloomingdales.com
- **SHEETS:** Charisma from Bloomingdale's, Bloomingdales.com
- **SIDE TABLES:** Cubitec from Design Within Reach, dwr.com
- **LAMPS:** Mitchell Gold and Bob Williams, mgandbw.com
- **BEDDING:** comforter from Bloomingdale's, Bloomingdales.com

THE MINIMAL BEDROOM
TINA ROTH EISENBERG, PAGES 150–151

- **BIG FRENCH POSTER:** Philip Williams Poster, postermuseum.com
- **PHOTOGRAPH:** Myoung Ho Lee, Lens Culture, Lensculture.com

OPPOSITE, CLOCKWISE FROM TOP LEFT: Alex McClain, Timothy and Laura Dahl, Tina Roth Eisenberg, Jennifer Ward, Maxwell Gillingham-Ryan, Hilary Padget and Anthony Harrington, Vané and Chad Broussard, Maxwell Gillingham-Ryan, Jen Chu.

THE FOUR-POSTER BEDROOM
JEN CHU, PAGES 152–155

- CHANDELIER: Brooklyn Flea, brooklynflea.com
- PAINT: Ralph Lauren from The Home Depot, homedepot.com
- HOOKS ON WALL: Ace Hardware, acehardware.com
- DESK: IKEA
- WALL LAMP: Restoration Hardware, restorationhardware.com
- FOUR-POSTER BED: custom
- NAIL HEADS: Martin Albert Interiors, martinalbert.com

THE PLATFORM BEDROOM
TIFFANY AND ALEX HILLKURTZ, PAGES 156–157

- LUMBER AND ALL SUPPLIES: The Home Depot, homedepot.com
- STAIRCASE: Arke Karina modular stairway kit, arkestairs.com

THE OFFICE BEDROOM
KATIE RYAN, PAGES 158–159

- RUG: Pakobel on eBay, stores.ebay.com/Pakobel-Rugs
- ART OVER DESK: Daniel Ingroff, danielingroff.com
- STOOL: garage sale

THE ALCOVE BEDROOM
ALEX McCLAIN, PAGES 160–163

- BED: Alex McClain
- SIDE TABLE: IKEA (cut down)
- WALL SHELF, LIGHTS, AND BEDDING: IKEA
- CURTAIN: made by McClain's sister; fabric, Jo-Ann Fabrics, joann.com
- WARDROBE: IKEA countertop and Pax wardrobe system
- PAINT: black chalkboard paint

THOUGHTS ON BEDROOM COLORS
JENNIFER WARD, PAGE 165

- CAMERAS: from road trips across the country
- BEDDING: Bed Bath & Beyond, bedbathandbeyond.com

BETHANY OBRECHT, PAGES 166–167

- BEDDING: Dwell Studio, dwellstudio.com; TJMaxx; IKEA
- CURTAINS: IKEA
- HEADBOARD: eBay, ebay.com

KELLY GIESEN, PAGE 171

- FABRIC-COVERED HEADBOARD: custom
- WALLPAPER: hand made of thousands of beads

THOUGHTS ON BATHROOMS
KELLY GIESEN, PAGE 174 BELOW

- SINK: French table from flea market, distressed painting, re-topped with marble and inset with Kohler sink, kohler.com

KELLY VAN PATTER, PAGE 175 LEFT

- SINK: vintage re-porcelained
- TILE: Bisazza off-white

LESLIE MASLOW AND ALAN DORSEY, PAGE 176

- ARCHITECTS: Delson or Sherman, delsonsherman.com

LESLIE MASLOW AND ALAN DORSEY, PAGE 177 TOP

- ARCHITECTS: Delson or Sherman, delsonsherman.com

STACI BILLIS, PAGES 178–179

- GRAY LIMESTONE TILE: Anne Sacks Luxor Gray limestone, annesacks.com
- WHITE MOSAIC TILE: glass mosaic tile in pearl white
- ¾" SQ. GREEN TILE: Bisazza glass mosaic from International Tile, 4436 21st Street, Long Island City, NY, 718.728.3100

- TUB: Duravit, duravit.com
- MAIN SINK: Porcher, porcher-us.com, with Elba wall-mounted lavatory faucet, La Toscana, latoscanacollection.com
- SHOWER: Elba thermostatic shower faucet, La Toscana, latoscanacollection.com
- TOILET: cadet one-piece elongated toilet with seat, American Standard, americanstandard-us.com
- VANITY: custom, shop-sprayed white with mirror top
- TUB FAUCET: Elba three hole roman tub faucet in polished chrome, La Toscana, latoscanacollection.com
- HAND SHOWER: deck mount hand shower, La Toscana, latoscanacollection.com
- LITTLE SINK: Aquababy series wall mounted porcelain with Whitehaus lux single-hole, single-lever lavatory, Lacava, lacava.com
- CABINETS: above toilet, IKEA

KELLY GIESEN, PAGES 180–181

- HARDWARE: kitchen deck faucet, Rohl, rohlhome.com
- MIRROR: old Venetian mirror, Center44, center44.com
- SHOWER CURTAIN: terrycloth curtain, Gracious Home, gracioushome.com
- TUB HARDWARE: California faucets, calfaucets.com
- TUB: original
- TILE: Calcutta gold marble tile, 18x18
- TOWEL RACKS AND BARS: Restoration Hardware, restorationhardware.com
- TOILET: Porcher, porcher-us.com
- GLASS: gluechip glass

JUAN MATIZ, PAGES 182–183

- TUB: Zuma, AF New York, afnewyork.com
- SINK AND FAUCET: Davinci, AF New York, afnewyork.com
- SHOWER HARDWARE: Dornbracht, dornbract.com/en
- SHOWERHEAD: Grohe, grohe.com

- GLASS DOOR: Cesana, AT New York, cesana.it/ing
- COUNTERTOP: Ceasarstone
- CABINET: custom with Valli and Valli hardware, vallivalli-us.com
- ALL OTHER HARDWARE: Valli and Valli

SMART HOME OFFICES
TINA ROTH EISENBERG, PAGES 184–185

- DESK: Hold Everything, now West Elm, westelm.com
- CHAIR: drummer's stool
- LAMP: MoMA, momastore.org
- POSTER: Japanese Gaku Ohsugi
- BOOKSHELF: Design Within Reach, dwr.com

KELLY VAN PATTER, PAGES 186–187

- FLOORING: Douglas Fir, sanded and stained
- CEILING FIXTURE: Smith and Hawken
- SHADES: Hunter Douglas solar screens, hunterdouglas.com
- ROLLING FILES AND CART: CB2, cb2.com
- WASTEPAPER BASKET: Kartell (umbrella stand), hivemodern.com
- RUNNER: Crate&Barrel, crateandbarrel.com
- TASK CHAIRS: vintage Italian, found in antiques store
- CLOCK: Conran, conran.com
- TASK LAMP: yard sale
- TOTEMS: Native American
- CLOCHE: Pottery Barn, potterybarn.com
- SQUARE VASE: Rosenthal
- SWIRLY VASES: from Nemadji, Minnesota
- TV RACK: Best Buy, bestbuy.com
- HANGING FILE: IKEA
- SMALL FLAT FILE: Bisley, bisleyusa.com

HILARY PADGET AND ANTHONY HARRINGTON, PAGE 187, RIGHT

- CHAIR: Eames Management Chair, roomandboard.com

DAVID ALHADEFF, PAGE 189

- DESK AND CHAIR: The Future Perfect, thefutureperfect.com
- LAMP: Kila, from IKEA

THE COMMAND STATION OFFICE
KELLY VAN PATTER, PAGES 190–193

- FLOORING: Douglas Fir, sanded and stained
- CEILING FIXTURE: Smith and Hawken
- SHADES: Hunter Douglas solar screens, hunterdouglas.com
- ROLLING FILES AND CART: CB2, cb2.com
- WASTEPAPER BASKET: Kartell (umbrella stand), hivemodern.com
- RUNNER: Crate&Barrel, crateandbarrel.com
- TASK CHAIRS: vintage Italian, found in antiques store
- CLOCK: Conran, conran.com
- TASK LAMP: yard sale
- TOTEMS: Native American
- CLOCHE: Pottery Barn, potterybarn.com
- SQUARE VASE: Rosenthal
- SWIRLY VASES: from Nemadji, Minnesota
- TV RACK: Best Buy, bestbuy.com
- HANGING FILE: IKEA
- SMALL FLAT FILE: Bisley, bisleyusa.com

THE WALK-IN CLOSET OFFICE
YIMING WANG AND XIAN ZHANG, PAGE 194–197

- DESK: solid wood door, Metropolitan Lumber, themetlumber.com
- SHELVES: solid wood planks, Metropolitan Lumber, themetlumber.com
- BOXES, LIGHTS, AND MIRROR: IKEA
- CHAIRS: Marcel Breuer copies found on street and at Brooklyn Flea, brooklynflea.com

THE MINI-LIBRARY OFFICE
LESLIE MASLOW AND ALAN DORSEY, PAGES 198–199

- ARCHITECT: Delson or Sherman Architects, delsonsherman.com
- CABINETS: bamboo plywood
- DESK: Corian, dupont.com
- FLOORING: cherry wood
- CHAIR: Eames Aluminum Management Chair

THE CURTAIN OFFICE
MANSON FUNG, PAGES 200–203

- TABLE, CHAIR, CABINET, LIGHTING: IKEA
- CURTAINS: poly-chiffon fabric
- ROD: copper plumbing rod painted white, inspired by shoji screens
- SOFA: Craigslist, craigslist.org
- CUSHIONS: Target, target.com
- TABLES: cardboard, made by Manson
- CHAIR: Eames replica from online seller

THE IKEA HACKER OFFICE
ALEX McCLAIN, PAGES 204–205

- **BIG IMAGE:** Alex McClain, photo blown up using Poster Razor, posterrazor.com
- **FRAMES:** IKEA
- **DESK:** Numerar countertop, IKEA
- **SIDE CABINET:** IKEA Lomen with IKEA wardrobe doors on top
- **TASK CHAIR:** Target, target.com
- **CHAIR LEGS:** IKEA

THE CORNER OFFICE
KELLY GIESEN, PAGES 206–207

- **TWO ETCHED BIRD DOORS FROM PARIS:** ABC Home, abchome.com
- **BENCH:** 77th Street Flea in New York; fabric, Manuel Canovas, manuelcanovas.com/en
- **LAMP:** flea market, spare parts
- **CD RACK:** found in Finland
- **LUCITE FRAMES:** Gracious Home, gracioushome.com
- **SMALL CHAIR:** flea market; recovered with fabric from MOOD, moodfabrics.com
- **TABLE:** mirrored side table, Gracious Home, gracioushome.com
- **PILLOW:** ABC Home, abchome.com
- **SHAG RUGS:** custom cut at ABC Home, abchome.com

THE SLIDING OFFICE
TINA EISENBERG, PAGES 208–211

- **DESK:** Hold Everything, now West Elm, westelm.com
- **CHAIR:** drummer's stool
- **LAMP:** MoMA, momastore.com
- **POSTER:** Japanese Gaku Ohsugi
- **BOOKSHELF:** Design Within Reach, dwr.com

A FEW MORE QUICK OFFICES
JUSTINA BLAKENEY, PAGE 214

- **DESK:** Pronomen kitchen countertop on Vika legs, IKEA

SHARON BORDAS AND DAMON HILL, PAGE 215

- **CHAIR:** Eames soft pad management chair copy from In Mode Home on La Brea, inmodehome.com

YIMING WANG AND XIAN ZHANG, PAGE 216, LEFT

- **BARS:** Grundtal, from IKEA

MAT SANDERS, PAGE 216–217, MIDDLE

- **DESK:** IKEA

LUIS CAICEDO, PAGE 217, ABOVE RIGHT

- **BACKDROP:** FLOR tile, flor.com

THOUGHTS ON DESK ORGANIZATION
JEN CHU, PAGE 219

- **NAIL HEADS:** Martin Albert Interiors, martinalbert.com
- **DESK:** IKEA

LUIS CAICEDO, PAGE 220

- **DESK:** Housing Works, housingworks.org
- **BACKSPLASH:** FLOR tile, flor.com

MARK ROBOHM AND STEPHANIE DOUCETTE, PAGES 222–223

- **DESK CHAIR:** found on street, Herman Miller, hermanmiller.com
- **CREDENZA:** found on street

JEN CHU, PAGE 224

- **NAIL HEADS:** Martin Albert Interiors, martinalbert.com
- **DESK:** IKEA

PETITE CHILDREN'S ROOMS
TINA ROTH EISENBERG, PAGES 226–227

- **ARTWORK:** Mareike Auer from The Shiny Squirrel, theshinysquirrel.com

ANDREA ROBBINS AND MAX BECHER, PAGE 228

- **RED CHAIR:** MoMA store, momastore.org
- **MUSHROOM LAMP:** Rose and Radish, roseandradish.com

KAREN GILLINGHAM, PAGE 230

- **LAMP:** Urban Outfitters, urbanoutfitters.com

MAXWELL AND SARA KATE GILLINGHAM-RYAN, PAGE 231

- **PILLOW:** Andrianna Shamaris, andriannashamaris.com

THE CAPSULE BUNK BED
ANDREA ROBBINS AND MAX BECHER, PAGES 232-235

- **BUNK BEDS:** custom
- **RED CHAIR:** MoMA store, momastore.org
- **MUSHROOM LAMP:** Rose and Radish, roseandradish.com

THE BREAKTHROUGH NURSERY
STEPHANIE DOUCETTE AND MARK ROBOHM, PAGES 236–239

- **CRIB AND TABLE:** Netto, nettocollection.com; Ebay, ebay.com
- **GRAY SHELVES:** purchased in Holland
- **RUG:** cowhide from Argentina
- **CABINET:** IKEA, found on street
- **CHAIR:** Jason Lewis, jasonlewisfurniture.com; recovered by Stephanie
- **BIG PHOTO:** DoucetteDuval photo shoot, doucetteduvall.com

THE ARCHITECTS' UNDER-NURSERY
SARA AND JUAN MATIZ, PAGES 240–243

- **BUILDER:** LNL Construction, lnlrenovation.com
- **CABINETS:** custom design with IKEA door and Valli and Valli handles, vallivalli-us.com
- **RUG:** FLOR tile, flor.com
- **CHAIRS:** Blu Dot, bludot.com
- **WALL MOUNT SLIDING:** Johnson Hardware, extruded aluminum, johnsonhardware.com
- **STAIRS:** custom metalwork
- **OUTER CABINETS:** IKEA doors and bodies wrapped in a custom frame
- **GLASS DIVIDER BY MASTER BED:** Channel Glass from Pilkington, Pilkington.com

THE PRINCESS ROOM
JENNIFER WARD, PAGES 244–249

- **BED:** IKEA
- **RUG:** Urban Outfitters, urbanoutfitters.com
- **BOOKCASE:** Bed Bath & Beyond, bedbathandbeyond.com
- **PICTURE WITH RAINBOW:** Cliff Richards wrapping paper
- **CURTAIN CANOPY:** ten panels with long curtain rods attached by socket to wall, IKEA
- **SHELF AND BIRDCAGE:** flea markets
- **BROOKLYN LETTERS:** Urban Outfitters, urbanoutfitters.com

THE ROOM-TO-GROW CHILDREN'S ROOM
TINA ROTH EISENBERG, PAGES 250–255

- BED, RUG, BEDDING, AND SHELF: IKEA
- SHELVES: Design Within Reach, dwr.com
- DESK: Picolino from Design Public, designpublic.com
- BINS: Container Store, containerstore.com
- BUNNY LAMP: POMME in Dumbo, pommenyc.com
- DOLLHOUSE: Melissa and Doug from Amazon, amazon.com
- DOLLS: Ugly Dolls, uglydolls.com
- TAXI DRAWING: James Rizzi, jamesrizzi.com
- LITTLE GIRL DRAWING: Camilla Engman, camillaengman.com
- RED GIRL ARTWORK: Mareike Auer from The Shiny Squirrel, theshinysquirrel.com
- BIG NUMBERS: Vintage Signage, 334 Atlantic Avenue, Brooklyn, NY 11201, 718.834.9268

THE LULU ROOM OF BIRDS
KAREN GILLINGHAM, PAGES 256–261

- PENDANT LAMP: www.lampsexpo.com
- RUG: Anthropologie, anthropologie.com
- BED: Purchased at garage sale in late '70s
- VINTAGE BASKET: American Rag/Maison Midi
- BIRD FABRICS: fabrics.com
- APPLIQUÉD PILLOWS: dishtowels from Anthropologie sewn onto pillows, anthropologie.com
- BIRD LAMP: Urban Outfitters, urbanoutfitters.com
- WALL HANGING: Bla Bla Kids, blablakids.com

THOUGHTS ON STORAGE
SARA KATE AND MAXWELL GILLINGHAM-RYAN, PAGE 265, BOTTOM RIGHT

- BLOCKS: Community Playthings, communityplaythings.com

THOUGHTS ON NURSERY LIGHTING
SARA KATE AND MAXWELL GILLINGHAM-RYAN, PAGES 268–269, 270, AND 271 (BOTTOM RIGHT)

- PAPER LANTERNS AND TWINKLE LIGHTS: Pearl River, pearlriver.com
- ARTWORK: designed by Maxwell Gillingham-Ryan
- CRIB AND DRESSER: IKEA
- MATTRESS: Eco Baby, purerest.com
- LAMP: Marre Moerel, marremoerel.com
- WALL HOOKS: antiques from flea market
- RUG: Overland Sheepskin Company, overland.com

THE LISTS

GREAT FOLDING CHAIRS

- High-end leather lends some sleekness to a seat.
  Lina Leather Folding Chair, dwr.com, $$$

- The Fol.d is a slick plastic number by Patrick Jouin.
  Fol.d Folding Chair, UnicaHome.com, zwello.com,
  $$$

- Jasper Morrison's Air Chair for Magis works inside or
  outdoors.
  Foldable Air Chair, Nova68.com, unicahome.com,
  or modlivin.com, $$$

- For a modern, barely-there look, try acrylic folding
  chairs.
  Search for "clarity acrylic folding chairs,"
  advancedinteriordesigns.com, bellacor.com, $$$

- Traditionalists may prefer craftsman-style folding
  chairs with padded seats.
  Search for "craftsman" and "slat back" folding
  chairs, plowandhearth.com, $$

- Folding bistro chairs are classic French café style.
  Search for "folding bistro chairs,"
  americancountryhomestore.com, $$

- Director's chairs, made from wood and canvas, are
  basic and comfortable.
  They're available in every possible color and size at
  directorschair.com, $

- Target carries decent folding chairs made from
  wood.
  Search "beechwood," "walnut," or "bamboo"
  folding chairs, target.com, $

- For wooden folding chairs on the cheap, IKEA is a
  good bet.
  Terje and Edgar folding chairs,
  Brommo deck chair, Ikea.com, $

OPPOSITE, CLOCKWISE FROM TOP LEFT: Juan and Sara Matiz,
Noah Posnick, Mat Sanders, Vanessa Ward and Brian Krex, Maxwell
Gillingham-Ryan, Katie Ryan, Kelly Giesen, Sara Kate, Ursula, and
Maxwell Gillingham-Ryan, Mark Robohm.

PAINT COLORS THAT COMPLEMENT A SMALL SPACE

- Dark browns usually make a small space feel cozy and cavelike.
  Galvanized (UL12) from Ralph Lauren is deep and dark, ralphlaurenhome.com

- For pale walls, misty gray-whites can evoke the open sky.
  Benjamin Moore's Horizon (OC-53) is cloudlike, benjaminmoore.com

- A deep gray adds a sense of mystery to a small room.
  Benjamin Moore's Witching Hour (2120-30) is an elegant slate color, benjaminmoore.com

- French blue is a saturated, unexpected color that feels crisp and clean.
  Ralph Lauren's Tulum Blue (IB88) is rich and jewel toned, ralphlaurenhome.com

- White is a standard color for small spaces, since it reflects light and tends to "open up" a space.
  Benjamin Moore's Decorators White (04) is a basic, cool-toned pure white, benjaminmoore.com

- Yellow can make a small room feel sunny if you choose the right shade and your room has good natural light.
  Farrow & Ball's Pale Hound (71) is a cool yellow that's recommended for small spaces, farrow-ball.com

- If you want to go bold, consider painting an accent wall to create a focal point.
  Farrow & Ball's Brinjal (222) is an unexpected, rich aubergine, farrow-ball.com

- In a really small space, like a bathroom or closet, you can go even bolder.
  Benjamin Moore's (2018-20) Mandarin Orange provides a super-strong jolt of color, benjaminmoore.com

GENERAL SPACE SAVERS

- Furniture that serves more than one purpose saves space and allows you to mix things up without making major changes.

- Recessed and track lighting frees up surface and floor space while creating a sense of expansion (especially when you aim spotlights at the walls).

- Wall-mounted shelving provides much-needed vertical space to store and access your stuff.

- Folding and collapsible furniture can come in handy when you have a dinner party and you need to add extra seating.

- Custom built-ins, within a home's existing nooks and crannies, offer storage without eating up valuable floor space.

- Low-profile and clean-lined furniture open up space by making walls and windows appear taller, creating a visually lightweight aesthetic.

- Wireless networking streamlines the amount of cables and cords on display, and reduces the number of bulky boxes you need to operate your home.

- Modular furniture can be customized to fit your space, even as you move from one home to another.

- Closet systems streamline your storage and help you stay organized. To create a place for everything, use a mix of hanging rods, hooks, shelving, and a shoe rack.

- Editing is the key to living well in a small space. Love everything you own, and weed out the rest.

GREAT EXPANDABLE DINING TABLES

- The Muddus Drop-Leaf Table is so tiny that it expands from a one-seater to a two-seater.
  Muddus Drop-Leaf Table, ikea.com, $

- The Packet Table and Chair Set transforms from a compact box into a four-seat dining set.
  Packet Table and Chairs, offi.com, $$

- Italian company Ozzio offers a wide range of expandable dining tables with a contemporary look.
  ozzio.com, $$$

- The basic Parsons Dining Table comes in an expandable version that seats between six and eight.
  Parsons Expandable Dining Table, westelm.com, $$

- If you're on a tight budget, search craigslist.org and thrift stores for secondhand finds.
  Search for "gateleg," "dropleaf," and "expandable" tables, craigslist.org, $

- The Norden Gateleg Table is a wooden drop-leaf model with built-in storage drawers. It seats two to four.
  Norden Gateleg Table, ikea.com, $

- Room and Board sells solid wood extension tables that seat anywhere from six to ten people.
  Search "extension table" roomandboard.com, $$–$$$

- Jensen & Lewis carries a broad line of extension tables, including several round versions.
  Search "extension table," jensen-lewis.com, $$$

- The Spanna Extension Table stores its leaves inside itself and opens up with a lift-and-slide mechanism, seating four to six.
  Spanna Extension Table, dwr.com, $$$

HOW TO HOUSE YOUR TV

- Camouflage a wall-mounted TV stand to match your decor.
  Muro Media Storage, dwr.com, $$$

- Integrate the TV into a media-friendly bookcase system.
  Modena Wall System, boconcept.com, $$$

- Use a triangular media stand to tuck the TV into a corner.
  Corner TV Entertainment Centers, racksandstands.com, $$

- Mount your TV on a panel system for a modern look that hides cords.
  Besta Storage & Framsta Panels, ikea.com, $$

- Create a custom surround using a mantelpiece or built-in cabinet.
  Search "Hide Your TV Monitor with Style, apartmenttherapy.com, $–$$$

- Frame a wall-mounted LCD or plasma TV.
  Invidia TV Frames, hdenvy.com, $$$

- Use a ceiling-mounted projector to replace your TV altogether.
  Projectors and fittings, optomausa.com, $$$

- Make a fabric cozy to hide your flatscreen.
  Search for "Holly's TV Cozy," apartmenttherapy.com, $

- A home theater cabinet stores your electronics in style.
  Search "cabinets," bdiusa.com, $$–$$$

HEADBOARDS AND BEDS

- Latticed headboards let in light through a small space.
  The Morocco, Window, and Overlapping Squares headboards are good bets, westelm.com, $$

- Save space with a wallpapered or painted headboard
  Custom wallpaper, designyourwall.com, $

- A comfortable daybed doubles as both sofa and bed.
  I like the Case Study Daybed, modernica.net, $$–$$$

- A mirrored headboard reflects light.
  Search "mirrored headboard," julianchichester.com, $$$

- Campaign and cottage beds are classic small space solutions.
  Search "brass" and "iron" beds, charlesprogers.com, $$

- Custom Murphy Beds are another compact standby.
  Search for a carpenter to build your bed, apartmenttherapy.com, $$–$$$

- The wall-mounted Mandal Headboard has adjustable shelves.
  Mandal Headboard, ikea.com, $

- A low platform bed makes ceilings seem higher.
  Search for "platform beds," designpublic.com, roomandboard.com, Ikea.com, $–$$$

- A tufted headboard creates a focal point in a small space.
  Search for "DIY tufted headboard," apartmenttherapy.com, $

- Backlight a headboard for a sense of drama.
  Use rope light and a staple gun, ledropelightsandmore.com, $

BOOKSHELVES FOR TIGHT SPACES

- Wall-mounted Vitsoe Shelving by Dieter Rams always looks timeless.
  606 Universal Shelving System, vitsoe.com, $$$

- Cubitec Shelving by Doron Lachish is modular and easy to reconfigure.
  Cubit and Cubitec Shelving, dwr.com, smartfurniture.com, $$

- The Elfa wall-mounted shelving system can be designed to fit your space.
  Elfa Shelving, containerstore.com, $$

- The String Pocket by Nisse Strinning is perfect for paperbacks.
  String Pocket, string.se, scandinaviandesigncenter.com, $$

- The Umbra Conceal Book Shelf makes your books seem as if they're floating on the wall.
  Conceal Book Shelf, umbra.com, $

- The Sapien Bookcase by Bruno Rainaldi is a tall shelf with a small footprint.
  Sapien Bookcase, dwr.com, $$

- The Vitra Self Shelves by Ronan and Erwan Bouroullec are colorful and adjustable.
  Self Shelves, vitra.com, $$$

- Jesper's Expando Shelving is made of open, L-shaped units that stack together.
  Expando Shelving, jesperoffice.com, $

- Ceiling-mounted shelving frees up floor space.
  Search "books in the rafters" and "wraparound ceiling shelving," apartmenttherapy.com, $–$$

- If you really want to get creative, build shelving into your staircase.
  Search "the amazing staircase," apartmenttherapy.com, $–$$$

WAYS TO DISPLAY ART

- Use a picture rail to hang your art.
  Search for "classic," "cable," and "click rail" systems, ashanging.com, $$

- Hang a grid of gallery frames.
  Wood Gallery Frames, potterybarn.com, $–$$

- Lean art along a modern picture ledge.
  Ribba Picture Ledge, ikea.com, $

- Cluster artwork in similar frames.
  We like the "Ribba" and the "Fjallsta" frames, ikea.com, $

- Cluster artwork in mismatched frames.
  Order custom sizes and styles online, americanframe.com, $$

- Hang textiles with a wall kit.
  Search for "wall hanging kits," txtlart.com, $–$$

- Illuminate paintings with picture lights.
  Search for "picture lights," croftandlittle.com, $$$

- Make a DIY photo blow-up.
  The "rasterbator" is a great online photo tiling tool, homokaasu.org/rasterbator, $

- Hang prints inexpensively with Jorgen Moller's Poster Hanger.
  It's a simple, glass-free system, posterhanger.com, $

- Convert a collection of plates into art.
  Search for "adhesive plate hanger," allplatehangers.com, $

TOP TABLE LAMPS FOR THE LIVING ROOM

- The Tolomeo Classic Lamp is a hard-working, adjustable task light.
  Tolomeo Classic Lamp, artemide.us, $$$

- The Miss K Lamp by Philippe Starck for FLOS is sleek and chic.
  Miss K Lamp, ylighting.com, $$$

- IKEA's Kulla table lamp is a basic, Bauhaus-inspired style.
  Kulla Table Lamp, ikea.com, $

- For a more traditional look, try a pharmacy-style task light.
  Atelier Table Lamp, restorationhardware.com, $$

- The Spun Table Lamp by Sebastian Wong is an ultra-cool, minimalist design of pressed glass.
  Spun Table Lamp, hivemodern.com, $$$

- Designed in 1930 by Robert Dudley Best, the Bestlite table lamp is a mixture of British and Bauhaus styles.
  Bestlite Table Lamp, unicahome.com, $$$

- The Haley Table Lamp has a sculptural, metallic base.
  Haley Table Lamp, crateandbarrel.com, $$

- The Ada Table Lamp is an inexpensive model that looks great in white-on-white.
  Ada Table Lamp, cb2.com, $

- For lighting that looks like paper sculpture, try one of Isamu Noguchi's classic table lamps.
  Noguchi Table Lamps, momastore.org, $$

- IKEA's Fado Lamp is a simple globe light that looks more expensive than it is.
  Fado Lamp, ikea.com, $

TOP TEN KITCHEN SPACE SAVERS

- Undershelf baskets double your available space.
  Search for "undershelf baskets,"
  containerstore.com, $

- Wall-mounted wine racks free up counter and floor space.
  Vintage View Wine Storage System,
  vintageview.com, $$

- Multi-purpose kitchen rails keep pots, pans, and utensils close at hand.
  Search for the "Grundtal" series, ikea.com, $

- Hanging pot racks suspend your pots and pans from the ceiling.
  Search "ceiling" or "hanging" pot rack,
  overstock.com, $–$$

- Folding tables with stackable stools are a great way to make space for dining in the kitchen.
  Norden Gateleg Table and Frosta Stools,
  ikea.com, $

- Stemware racks and mug hooks free up valuable cabinet and counter space.
  Search "stemware rack" and "cup or mug holders,"
  spacesavers.com, $

- Magnetic spice and knife racks keep things organized on the wall.
  Search "magnetic rack," cooking.com, $–$$

- See-through storage creates a sense of order in your pantry.
  OXO Good Grips POP Containers, oxo.com,
  crateandbarrel.com, $$

- Mini and oversink dish racks won't eat up all your counter space.
  Search "compact" and "over the sink" dish racks,
  bedbathandbeyond.com, simplehuman.com, $–$$

- Small-scale rolling kitchen carts add movable counter space.
  Metro Commercial Chef's Cart,
  containerstore.com, $$

SMALL COOL DESKS

- The IKEA PS Laptop workstation is an inexpensive, space-saving design that mounts to the wall.
  IKEA PS Laptop workstation, ikea.com, $

- The Overlap Tray is a portable laptop desk made of molded plywood.
  Offi Overlap Tray, offi.com, $$

- The LAX wall-mounted desk by MASH Studios is modern and streamlined.
  LAX Collection by MASH
  designpublic.com, atworkdesign.com,
  allmodern.com, $$$

- George Nelson's swag leg design is a classic small-space writing desk with graceful curves.
  Nelson Swag Leg Desk, roomandboard.com, $$$

- Atlas Shelving offers wall-mounted wooden desk and shelving systems in an organic modern style.
  AS4 Shelving, atlaseast.com, $$$

- The Convertible Compact Desk transforms from a cabinet to a full-sized desk.
  Convertible Compact Desk, crateandbarrel.com, $$

- The Waveform by John Paul Plauche is a minimal wall-mounted desk made of sheet metal.
  Waveform, flukecollective.com, $$

- The Parsons Desk is a simple, rectangular form that goes with almost any style.
  Parsons Mini Desk, westelm.com, $

- Leaning, ladderlike desks have a small footprint, and they're generally inexpensive.
  Search for "leaning desk," roomandboard.com,
  crateandbarrel.com, $

- Jasper Morrison's NesTable is an adjustable and ergonomic laptop stand.
  NesTable, vitra.com, $$$

OPEN STORAGE SOLUTIONS

- Make a statement in your entryway with eye-catching hooks.
  Tom Dixon's Wire Coatrack is an Apartment Therapy favorite, dwr.com, $$$

- Small-scale, wall-mounted mail sorters and key catches are great for a small hallway.
  Search for "entry hall accessories," chiasso.com, $$

- Hang your bike on the wall to create functional storage and a Dadaist display.
  Cycloc Hanging System, cycloc.com, $$

- Open up your kitchen shelving for a casual, help-yourself atmosphere.
  Search "open kitchen shelving," apartmenttherapy.com, $–$$$

- Pegboard organizers can be used anywhere from the kitchen to the office.
  Search "pegboard," apartmenttherapy.com, $

- Desktop collators keep files and papers organized and in sight.
  Search for "desktop collator," russellandhazel.com, officesupplies.us.com, libertyoffice.com, $–$$

- Wall-mounted office organizers free up floor and surface space.
  Vitra Uten Silo, velocity.com, designpublic.com, vitra.com, $$$

- Vintage industrial-style open shelving works well in a kitchen, office, or entryway.
  Search "vintage," "industrial," or "metal" storage, rehabvintage.com, salvageone.com, $$–$$$

- Train racks are a compact, long-standing solution for bathroom storage.
  Search "bathroom train rack," restorationhardware.com, $$–$$$

- Use wall-mounted shoe racks to keep your collection organized and easily visible.
  Elfa Gliding Shoe Rack, containerstore.com, $$

- Open shelves can double as room dividers, letting light filter through.
  We like the Bamboo Stagger Shelves by Brave Space, bravespacedesign.com, $$$

TOP TEN MIRRORS

- The wood-rimmed Stave Mirror is a straightforward and inexpensive solution.
  Stave Mirror, ikea.com, $

- Infinity mirrors are "frameless" pieces that seem to blend into the wall.
  Aluminum-Framed Infinity Mirror, cb2.com, $

- The Matera Mirror is a substantial, modern piece with a solid walnut frame.
  Matera Mirror, dwr.com, $$$

- A freestanding, three-panel mirror brings glamour to a space as a dressing room divider.
  Three-Panel Floor Mirror, horchow.com, $$$

- For the perfect fit, seek out made-to-measure, customizable mirrors.
  Search for "custom mirrors," roomandboard.com $$–$$$

- A mirrored cabinet provides built-in storage behind a reflective surface.
  Search for "mirror cabinet," westelm.com, $$

- Chiasso's Runway Mirror is banded in wood veneer along the edges.
  Runway Mirror, chiasso.com, $

- Framed in oak, long mirrors have a sense of heft.
  Search for "oak mirror," lekkerhome.com, $$$

- Ornate frames made of hard shells, stones, and metal bring some texture to a space.
  Search for "mirrors," olystudio.com, $$$

- A Cheval-style, floor-length mirror is mounted on two hinges that swivel.
  Search for "cheval mirror," crateandbarrel.com, jcpenney.com, $–$$$

WAYS TO UNTANGLE YOUR WIRES

- Go wireless with network routers that link your computer, sound, and TV systems.
  Airport Express, apple.com, $$

- Wrangle cords cheaply with velcro wraps.
  Search for "velcro wraps" or "velcro ties," amazon.com, cableorganizer.com, staples.com, $

- Corral cables with sleek desktop organizers.
  SpaceStation, CableBox, bluelounge.com, $$

- To hide power strips and cables, mount them on the underside of a desk.
  Search for "cable management" or "how to hide cables," unplggd.com, $

- Streamline your entryway with a charging station you can make on your own.
  Search "DIY charging station," unplggd.com, $

- Use cord concealers to cover wires against a wall.
  Search for "cord concealers," amazon.com, containerstore.com, $

- Use wire looms to hide cables in a tube.
  Search for "wire looms" or "cable snakes," cableorganizer.com, $

- Opt for portable computing and minimal cords with a slim laptop.
  Search for "top ten ultra portable laptops," unplggd.com, $$$

- Buy furniture with built-in cord control.
  Studio Desk, bluelounge.com, $$

- Use nail-in clips to secure cords to a wall or desk.
  Search for "nail in clips," radioshack.com, amazon.com, $

acknowledgments

MY THANKS AND GRATITUDE TO:

All the people within these pages for opening your homes, putting up with long days of shooting, and believing that by sharing your homes you'd help others.

Jim Franco for helping translate my vision of a compendium of inspiring homes into gorgeous photographs. Joe Maer for bringing out the best of what was already in each home. And we couldn't have done any of the work on the road without Rich Vassilatos.

Valerie Rains for her patience, skilled editing, and graceful weaving together of the images and words.

Cambria Bold for keeping us all on track, and keeping all the hundreds of photographs organized from the very beginning to the very end of the project.

Aliza Fogelson at Potter for painstakingly editing all the odds and ends I brought back from my travels.

Kate Lee at ICM for watching over me, and Sara Marino at Apartment Therapy for watching out for me.

Sarah Coffey and Beth Neato for their awesome research Sarah's especially great lists bring an online experience to the printed page.

Karen Gillingham for building an amazing room for Ursula and being an indispensable sounding board.

Sara Kate and Ursula for loving my crazy plans.

the homeowners

David Alhadeff
Williamsburg, Brooklyn
Modern design store owner, The Future
Perfect
www.thefutureperfect.com

Stacie Billis and Michael Lebowitz
Clinton Hill, Brooklyn
Stacie: Parenting and Food writer,
www.chowmama.com
Michael Lebowitz: CEO, Big Spaceship

Justina Blakeney
Silver Lake Adjacent, Los Angeles
Designer, author, editor
www.justfordesign.com

Sharon Bordas and Damon Hill
3rd Street or Beverly Hills Adjacent,
Los Angeles
Married writing team

Vané and Chad Broussard
Brooklyn Heights, Brooklyn
Vané: Interior designer
Chad: Architectural designer

Luis Caicedo
Hell's Kitchen, Manhattan
Interior and product designer
www.luiscaicedo.com

Jen Chu
Fort Greene, Brooklyn
Set designer and decorator

Laura and Timothy Dahl
West Los Angeles
Timothy: founder of Charles and Hudson,
www.charlesandhudson.com
Laura: fashion designer, www.lauradahl.com

Stephanie Doucette and Mark Robohm
Chelsea, Manhattan
Mark: Drummer
Stephanie: Dress designer

Tina Roth Eisenberg and Gary Eisenberg
(and daughter Ella Joy)
Cobble Hill, Brooklyn
Tina: Graphic designer, blogger
Gary: Kitchen designer

Manson Fung
Hollywood, Los Angeles
Designer

Kelly Giesen
Upper West Side, Manhattan
Designer
www.kellyg-design.com

Sara Kate and Maxwell Gillingham-Ryan
West Village, Manhattan
Sara Kate: Food writer
Maxwell: Interior designer, blogger

Tiffany and Alex Hillkurtz
North Hollywood, Los Angeles
Tiffany: film editor
Alex: Illustrator

Leslie Maslow and Alan Dorsey
Carroll Gardens, Brooklyn
Leslie: Writer
Alan: Cabinetmaker and wood artist

Sara and Juan Matiz
Chelsea, Manhattan
Architects, Hangar Design Group NY
www.hangardesigngroup.com

Alex McClain
Historical Downtown Core, Los Angeles
Photographer
www.ampphoto.com

Michelle and Tracy McCormick
Wilshire District, Los Angeles
Michelle: Design director, Forever 21
Tracy: Senior Project manager, Gary Gibson
Studio

Bethany Obrecht
Brooklyn Heights, Brooklyn
Partner, Found My Animal
www.foundmyanimal.com

Hilary Padget and Anthony Harrington
Fort Greene, Brooklyn
Architects and partners at pHdesign
www.phdesign.us

Noah Posnick
Greenwich Village, Manhattan
Commercial director

Andrea Robbins and Max Becher
Soho, Manhattan
Artists and professors
www.robbinsbecher.com

Katie Ryan
Mt. Washington, Los Angeles
Artist/designer

Mat Sanders
West Village, New York
Writer/performer

Kelly Van Patter
Highland Park, Los Angeles
Green interior designer and production
designer
www.vanpatterdesign.com

Yiming Wang and Xian Zhang
Hell's Kitchen, Manhattan
Yiming: Photographer
Xian: Financial manager at Morgan Stanley

Jennifer Ward (and daughter Parker Chinn)
Carroll Gardens, Brooklyn
Founder, imagination agent and creative
director of Minor Details Design
www.minordetails.typepad.com

Vanessa Ward and Brian Krex
Upper West Side, Manhattan
Brian: Lawyer
Vanessa: Writer

index